APSLEY HOUSE
WELLINGTON MUSEUM

Simon Jervis & Maurice Tomlin
Revised by Jonathan Voak

VICTORIA & ALBERT MUSEUM

First published by the
Victoria and Albert Museum,
London, 1984
Revised 1989, 1995.

The Victoria and Albert Museum
London SW7 2RL

© The Trustees of the
Victoria and Albert Museum 1984, 1995

ISBN 1 85177 161 1

Photography by Ken Jackson,
Jeremy Whitaker, Richard Bryant

The drawings illustrated on pages 6 and 43
are reproduced by permission of the
Trustees of Sir John Soane's Museum.

First edition designed by
Leonard Lawrance

Printed in Italy

Front cover
Apsley House

Frontispiece
Arthur Wellesley, First Duke of Wellington
(1769-1852) by Sir Thomas Lawrence,
P.R.A., about 1815

Back cover
Apsley House
Lithograph by J Dillon; 1853
On the front of the building can be seen
the shadow of the equestrian statue of
Wellington which stood previously on the
Constitution Hill Arch.

FOREWORD

Apsley House was offered to the Nation in 1947 by the Seventh Duke of Wellington in one of the most outstanding acts of generosity this century. The Government gratefully accepted the offer which comprised the House and much of its contents under the terms of the Wellington Museum Act of 1947. The contents included the magnificent collection of paintings, porcelain, plate, sculpture, orders and decorations, furniture and personal relics. Provision was also made for the Wellington family to retain apartments, happily maintaining their historic association with the House.

The Wellington Museum, Apsley House, first opened to the public on 19 July 1952. The Museum and collections are administered by the Victoria and Albert Museum and the Department of National Heritage is responsible for the maintenance of the building. From 1992-1995 the House was closed for major building and refurbishment works, which included the replacement of the electrical and heating systems, the overhaul of the roof and installation of a new air handling plant to improve the environment for the priceless collections. In line with Museum policy the opportunity has also been taken to return the interior of the House, as far as possible, to its appearance in the time of the First Duke. Unicorn Consultancy, the project manager appointed by the Department of National Heritage, has worked closely with the Curator of Apsley House and the specialists at the Victoria and Albert Museum to maintain historical accuracy. The conservation of the House and its outstanding collections is a continuing process.

This is the second revision of the guide book which was first published in 1984 and is a distant successor to the pamphlet guide issued by the Second Duke of Wellington in 1853. It also owes much to the guide book by Charles Gibbs-Smith published to coincide with the opening of the Museum in 1952 and revised through seven editions by Victor Percival MBE, Officer-in-Charge from 1947-1981. The authorship of the present guide is shared between Simon Jervis, responsible for Apsley House from 1976-1987 and Maurice Tomlin, Officer-in-Charge from 1981-1986 and has been revised by Jonathan Voak, Curator from 1987, to incorporate the extensive changes and improvements made during the recent refurbishment.

As a consequence of the widespread destruction of the great town houses and the dispersal of their collections, Apsley House now stands alone. With its collections largely intact and the family in residence, it is the most complete aristocratic town house in London. Described in 1908 as the "most renowned mansion in the capital", Apsley House survived when most others did not due to the foresight and munificence of the Seventh Duke of Wellington.

I remain deeply grateful to the present Duke of Wellington for his encouragement of our efforts to promote Apsley House and the achievements of the First Duke.

Elizabeth Esteve-Coll
Director
Victoria and Albert Museum

APSLEY HOUSE

Arms of the Duke of Wellington, from the Prussian Service, Berlin porcelain, about 1819

View of Hyde Park Corner showing Apsley House, about 1900. Frances Frith Collection

Apsley HOUSE was built between 1771 and 1778 for the second Earl of Bathurst (1714-1794). It takes its name from the title, Baron Apsley (created 1771), he held before succeeding his father as Earl Bathurst in 1775. It was designed by the neo-classical architect Robert Adam (1728-1792), many of whose designs for the building and its decoration and furniture are preserved in Sir John Soane's Museum. The house was originally faced in red brick and comprised five bays. Built on the site of a lodge to Hyde Park, it was the first house to be encountered after passing the toll gates at the top of Knightsbridge, a conspicuous position which must be responsible for its popular nickname, 'No. 1 London'.

In 1807 Apsley House was bought by the Marquess Wellesley (1760-1842) from the third Earl Bathurst for £16,000. Wellesley, the First Duke of Wellington's elder brother, had returned from India in 1805 a wealthy man, and employed the fashionable architect James Wyatt (1746-1813), assisted by Thomas Cundy (1765-1825), to carry out alterations and improvements. By 1816 Wellesley was in pecuniary difficulties and it was fortunate for him that he was able in 1817 to sell Apsley House to his brother for £42,000.

Wellington had then returned from duties as Ambassador to France, with a dazzling reputation as a soldier and with a political career in view. He was advised on the purchase by his former secretary, the architect Benjamin Dean Wyatt (1775-1850), son of James Wyatt. In 1818 Benjamin Dean Wyatt carried out repairs and installed the Canova statue of Napoleon. In 1819 he built the classical Dining Room in the North-East corner, where the Waterloo Banquets were held from 1820 to 1829.

In about 1827 the Duke of Wellington seems to have set aside any plans to build a Waterloo palace with the £200,000 voted him by Parliament, and determined to enlarge Apsley House into a London residence appropriate to his status and collections. Benjamin Dean Wyatt was therefore employed to enlarge the house by two bays to the West, incorporating a great picture gallery, to add a Corinthian portico, and to encase the whole in Bath stone. The entrance screen and gates were replanned at the same time, to accord with the adjoining Ionic Hyde Park Screen designed by Decimus Burton (1800-1881) in about 1825. (In 1982 the iron gates and railings were repainted the original bronze-green colour.) For the interior of the new gallery Wyatt employed the Lous XIV or 'Versailles' style of ornament, which his brother Matthew Cotes Wyatt (1777-1862) had pioneered at Belvoir Castle in 1824, and which he himself used at York House (later Stafford House, and now Lancaster House) from 1825.

By 1831 the Duke had spent about £64,000 on improvements, an expense about which he complained bitterly. Plasterwork was carried out by the firms of Bernasconi and George Jackson & Sons; metalwork was supplied by

Design for the ceiling of the second drawing-room (the Portico Drawing Room) by Robert Adam, 1775. Sir John Soane's Museum

J. Bramah & Sons and furniture by Thomas Dowbiggin & Co. Dowbiggin's successors, Holland & Sons, carried out the arrangements for the Duke's funeral in 1852 and made an inventory of Apsley House in 1854. The Second Duke of Wellington (1807-1884) allowed the public to visit the principal apartments of the house from 1853 onwards; they were open three days a week, but admission was allowed only in answer to written application. The Second Duke made some alterations on the ground floor but the main rooms remained substantially intact until the house was presented to the nation by the Seventh Duke of Wellington (1885-1972) in 1947. In World War II a bomb and a flying bomb had fallen nearby: their damage and the effects of time were put right by a major renovation carried out by the Ministry of Public Building and Works in time for the public opening on July 19th 1952. In 1961 to 1962 a road was built to the East, separating the House from Piccadilly. The new east façade was then faced with Bath stone and pierced with windows, the coach house removed and the forecourt rendered symmetrical.

View of Hyde Park Corner (with Apsley House in the foreground) by Edward Dayes, 1810

The Refurbishment of Apsley House

In recent years much has been done to return Apsley House, in so far as possible, to its appearance during the occupancy of the First Duke of Wellington. The process was initiated by the Victoria and Albert Museum and started with the restoration of the Portico Room in 1978. Work followed in the Piccadilly Room (1980), the Waterloo Gallery (1980), Plate and China Room (1981), Staircase (1982) and Dining Room (1982). The House was closed from 1992-1995 for major building and refurbishment works, which included the replacement of the electrical and heating systems, the overhaul of the roof, the installation of a new air handling plant to improve the environment for the priceless collections, and modern fire and safety systems. This provided the opportunity to completely refurbish the interiors, paying special attention to the Yellow and Striped Drawing Rooms, Entrance and Inner Halls.

Restoration work has taken account of the inventories of the House of 1854 and 1857, surviving bills, published accounts by Richard Ford and others and early photographs and watercolours of the interiors. Physical research has included the examination, both internally and externally, of paint sections to discover original colours and finishes. The shade of green on the exterior railings dating from 1829, was found as a result of this investigation. Paint sections were also analyzed from each of the Entrance Halls to establish the character of the marbling and the position of the block lines. Surviving fragments of the original carpets and wall-hangings have in most cases allowed their accurate reproduction. Where evidence is insufficient or unavailable, an attempt has been made to follow appropriate contemporary models. However, wherever original decorative surfaces remained, great care has been taken to retain and conserve them. For instance, much of the original gilding has survived and cleaning has revealed it to be in good condition. The elaborate parquet floor of the Waterloo Gallery has been repaired and its character, the result of a century and a half of use, preserved.

Although the aim of the Museum has been to return the building to its appearance as the private palace of the First Duke, alterations made by subsequent Dukes have been respected and care taken to maintain a sense of the development of the House over two centuries. For example, the cast iron radiator covers and mosaic floors in the Entrance Halls installed by the Second Duke have been retained.

Fragment of original carpet c. 1828-30

In the Striped and Yellow Drawing Rooms the modern fabric for the wall hangings had to be replaced. A small piece of the original hangings from the Yellow Room had survived and the fabric was copied by hand using wooden looms dating from the 1820s, the method used to produce the original 21″ wide fabric. Once the yellow striped taboret had been completed, the loom was loaded with crimson and buff dyed silk to produce the fabric for the Striped Drawing Room. It was also decided to make curtains for both rooms and, in the Striped Drawing Room, banquette seating and a central ottoman as shown in an 1852 watercolour of the room by Thomas Shotter Boys. In total, over 300 metres of fabric was woven.

The First Duke's gilded iron picture chain, complete with fittings, has been re-used to hang his extensive collection of paintings. In some rooms it has been possible to reproduce the arrangement adopted by the First Duke, thereby reflecting his preferences and the prevailing taste. The present arrangement in the Striped Drawing Room replicates, as far as possible, that shown in the 1852 watercolour. Although this type of decorative scheme in which paintings are hung in tiers was common in great London houses in the 19th century, it is rare to find it today.

Fortunately, examples of curtain rails, French pulley rods, door and window handles and all other brass accessories had survived to enable exact copies to be made where items were missing. Similarly, it was possible to have new glass blown and cut in order to restore the chandeliers to their former glory. New pieces were only made when it could be established exactly what was missing and they have been etched with the date of manufacture to distinguish them from the original 19th century glass.

Completing the refurbishment is the new carpet which has been woven to resemble as closely as possible a surviving piece of the original carpet which was discovered in the attics of Stratfield Saye, the Duke of Wellington's country house. Like the approach taken elsewhere, the reproduction of the carpet has been uncompromising. The replica is a woollen Brussels loop pile carpet, woven in 27″ widths and dyed to match unfaded threads drawn from the original fragment.

Fragment of original yellow taboret c. 1828-30

The Inner Hall

*The Seventh Duke of Wellington, K.G.,
by Peter Greenham, R.A. Lent by
His Grace the Duke of Wellington*

The Inner Hall, described thus in the 1854 Inventory and as the Waiting Hall leading to Grand Staircase (sic) in the 1857 Inventory, was remodelled by Wyatt in about 1830; before then it was the entrance hall. The ceiling is plain, the walls are painted to resemble Siena marble, and the doors are mahogany. The mosaic floor, along with the cast-iron radiator covers, was probably installed by the Second Duke of Wellington in about 1860. The three French mahogany side-tables with gilt-bronze mounts and granite tops date from about 1810 and were in this room under the First Duke along with, among other items, 'a hexagon lantern with three burners... a Pembroke- and a sofa-table and 2 mahogany chairs with leather seats'. The bronze statuette of Prince von Blücher (1742-1819) by Christian Daniel Rauch (1777-1857) is a reduction of Rauch's destroyed monument to Blücher set up in Breslau in 1827: it was probably in the Inner Hall under the First Duke, along with other bronzes and many marble busts. Now present are marble busts of the Duke of Wellington by Joseph Nollekens (1737-1823), 1813, Colonel John Gurwood, C.B., by Samuel Joseph (1791-1850), 1840, Sir Frederick Cavendish Ponsonby, K.C.B., (sculptor unknown), and the Duke of Wellington by George Gamon Adams (1821-1898), 1859.

On the north wall may be seen a state portrait by Peter Greenham R.A., painted in about 1952, of the Seventh Duke of Wellington (1885-1972), who gave Apsley House to the nation in 1947. The Seventh Duke succeeded to the title on the death of his nephew in action in 1943. As Lord Gerald Wellesley he had become an authority on artistic matters, serving as Surveyor of the King's Works of Art from 1936 to 1943. A particular interest was the Regency period and he was one of the leaders of the Regency Revival of the 1930s, as writer, collector and architect. He was an expert on his great-grandfather, the first Duke, publishing an *Iconography* (1935) and editing his letters (1965). The Seventh Duke also served as a Trustee of the National Gallery and as a member of the Advisory Council of the Victoria and Albert Museum.

*Overpage: The Battle of Waterloo,
by Felix Philipotteaux, 1874.
Victoria and Albert Museum*

The Inner Hall, about 1900

11

Prince von Blücher, by
Christian Daniel Rauch.
Bronze, 1824.

The paintings are as follows:

NORTH WALL

The Seventh Duke of Wellington K.G. (1885-1972)
By Peter Greenham R.A.
Lent by His Grace the Duke of Wellington.

The Duke of Wellington.
By Spiridone Gambardella (?1815-1856).
After a portrait by Lawrence, about 1825, now at Wellington College.

EAST WALL

Joseph Bonaparte, King of Spain (1768-1844).
By Baron Françoise Pascal-Gerard (1770-1837).
Signed F. Gerard.
Eldest brother of Napoleon. Defeated by Wellington at the Battle of Vitoria,
1813.

William Henry West Betty, the 'Young Roscius' (1791-1874).
Artist unknown. British school, about 1805.
Famous juvenile actor.

Passage of the Danube before the Battle of Wagram.
By Jacques François Joseph Swebach, called Fontaine (or Swebach-Desfontaines)
(1769-1823).

WEST WALL

Joseph Bonaparte, King of Spain (1768-1844).
By Robert Lefèvre (1755-1830).
Eldest brother of Napoleon. Defeated by Wellington at the Battle of Vitoria,
1813.

Alexander I, Emperor of Russia (1777-1825).
By George Dawe, R.A. (1781-1829).

The Duke of Wellington visiting the Outposts at Soignies.
By Hippolyte Lecomte (1781-1857). Signed.
Soignies, between Waterloo and Brussels, was the site of the British camp
in 1815.

The Hall

*The Duke of Wellington, by
Benedetto Pistrucci, 1832*

The Hall, described as the Front Hall in the 1854 Inventory and as the Entrance
Hall in the 1857 Inventory, was created by Wyatt in about 1830, when he moved
the entrance one bay westward. The ceiling is plain, the walls and columns are
painted to resemble Siena marble, and the doors are mahogany. As in the Inner
Hall the mosaic floor and radiator covers were probably installed by the Second
Duke of Wellington in about 1860, along with the black marble fireplace. Under
the First Duke the contents included 'a hexagon lantern with 3 burners... 6 hall
chairs, a porter's chair, a kneehole writing-table and an eight-day bracket clock'.
The Hall contains the following busts: the Duke of Wellington by Benedetto
Pistrucci (1784-1855), heroic size, 1832, by Sir Francis Chantrey, R.A. (1781-
1841), 1823, and by Sir John Steell (1804-1891), 1846, the Marquess of
Londonderry, K.G., by Chantrey, George Canning by Joseph Nollekens, R.A.
(1737-1823), Napoleon Bonaparte by A. Triscornia (1797-1867) after Canova,
and Richard, Marquess Wellesley, K.G., by John Francis (1780-1861), 1818, after
Nollekens, and a once-celebrated first century B.C. bust of Cicero from the
Mattei collection, which the Duke purchased in 1816. On the east wall is a
plaque erected in 1930 to commemorate the visit of the Venezuelan patriot
Simon Bolivar (1783-1830) in 1810 to the Marquess Wellesley, then Foreign
Secretary.

The paintings are as follows:

WEST WALL

His Last Return from Duty.
By James W. Glass (1825-1857).
Signed and dated 1853.
The Duke is shown riding from his office at the Horse Guards for the last time
as Commander-in-Chief.

The Battle of Waterloo.
By Felix Philipotteaux (1815-1884).
Historical reconstruction painted in 1874.

The Duke of Wellington.
By John Simpson (1782-1847).

EAST WALL

The Waterloo Banquet at Apsley House of 1836.
By William Salter.
Signed and dated 1840.
Lent by His Grace the Duke of Wellington.

The Waterloo Banquets at Apsley House

Dominating the entrance Hall is the painting by William Salter of the Waterloo Banquet which took place in the Waterloo Gallery at Apsley House in 1836.

Held annually by the First Duke of Wellington for the officers who served him at Waterloo, the Banquet took place at Apsley House from around 1820 until his death in 1852. It was a major social occasion and always attracted a large crowd outside the House, anxious to catch sight of the Iron Duke and his distinguished guests, including the Prince Consort. The first Waterloo Banquet was probably held in the new Dining Room in 1820. The early occasions were not the glamorous affairs of later years. The table in the new Dining Room could seat only 35, and the Duke necessarily restricted the guests to those senior officers who had fought on the battlefield at Waterloo.

Following the building of the Waterloo Gallery, which was completed in 1830, the Duke held the event there, as depicted by William Salter. The silver-gilt Portuguese Centrepiece had pride of place on the table (see p.63) and can be seen in the painting. Sideboards at each end of the Gallery were loaded with gold and silver plate and the great dinner and dessert services presented to the Duke by the sovereigns of Europe were put to use. At one end was displayed the silver-gilt Wellington Shield (shown in the painting) designed by Thomas Stothard who also designed the Waterloo Vase which stood on the sideboard at the opposite end. The Vase and Shield are on display in the Plate and China Room.

Up to 85 guests were seated at the Waterloo Banquets which were attended only by men. After the banquets had moved to the Waterloo Gallery, guests who had not been present at the Battle were also invited. Guests arrived between 6.30 pm and 7.30 pm and were greeted in the Entrance Hall by the band of the Grenadier Guards. The Duke, attired in the uniform of Colonel in the Grenadier Guards, came out to meet his guests under the Portico. As dessert was put on the table, the Duke would rise to propose a toast to the Queen, after which the band played the national anthem. This is the moment captured by William Salter. He shows Wellington addressing his fellow officers and other guests across the magnificent Portuguese plateau now on display in the Dining Room.

The Waterloo Banquet at Apsley House of 1836, by William Salter, 1840

The Plate and China Room

The Waterloo Vase, silver gilt, London 1824-25, designed by Thomas Stothard

Under the First Duke of Wellington, the Plate and China Room occupied the north-west corner of Apsley House. After his death in 1852 the Second Duke moved the room to its present position in the south-west corner, sweeping away some small ground-floor bedrooms to create the space. The new room had a very similar character to its predecessor, and the Second Duke moved his father's rosewood showcases in, adapting one to incorporate the door. He also installed the black marble fireplace. In 1981 new showcases were introduced, two in the outer window bays in the west wall, and a carpet was laid, woven to resemble that in interior watercolours of 1852 and 1853. In 1854 the room, sometimes called the Museum, contained, as well as many of the objects shown now, the Portuguese centre-piece (see p.63), bronze busts of Turenne and Condé, now at Stratfield Saye, two Indian drums, and a 'Wax Bust of the Duke on japan'd pedestal stand and glass shade'.

The large showcase on the north wall contains the Wellington Shield, designed by Thomas Stothard, R.A. (1755-1834) and made by Benjamin Smith for Green, Ward & Green in about 1822. Its central group, Wellington crowned by Victory, is surrounded by ten reliefs of scenes from his career. Flanking the Shield are Standard Candelabra by Benjamin Smith, dated 1816 to 1817. These are supported by figures of a Sepoy, a Portuguese soldier, and a Spanish guerilla (left) and an English, a Scottish, and an Irish soldier (right). Shield and Candelabra were presented to the Duke by the Merchants and Bankers of the City of London.

The Plate and China Room, watercolour by Thomas Shotter Boys, 1853

19

The rosewood case (1981) in the centre of the room contains the Sèvres Egyptian Service, purchased from the present Duke of Wellington by the Victoria & Albert Museum in 1979. The Service was made by the Sèvres porcelain factory from 1809 to 1812 as a divorce present from Napoleon to the Empress Josephine. She rejected it and in 1818 it was presented to Wellington by Louis XVIII of France. The book on Egypt (1802) by Dominique Vivant Denon (1747-1825) supplied the models for the monumental centre-piece, based on the Temples of Karnak, Dendera, and Philae, and for the views on the sixty-six plates. Three large cases on the east and south walls contain part of an even larger service made by the Berlin porcelain factory from 1816 to 1819 and presented to Wellington by King Frederick William III of Prussia (1770-1840). The sixty-four plates of this Prussian Service depict the Duke's life and campaigns, while its centre-piece includes a green porcelain obelisk with his orders and titles, and white

Plate from the Egyptian Service, Sèvres porcelain, painted by J.-F.-J. Swebach, with a view of the Sphinx, 1811

Vase from the Prussian Service, Berlin porcelain, about 1819

Ice-cream pail from the Egyptian Service,
Sèvres porcelain, painted and gilt by
Micaud, 1811

The Wellington Shield, designed by Thomas Stothard and made by Benjamin Smith, 1822, Detail

Part of the centrepiece from the Egyptian Service, Sèvres porcelain, 1809 to 1812

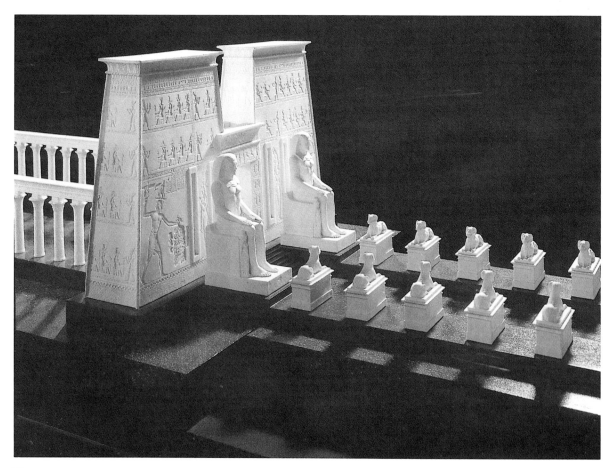

Figure of Britannia from the Prussian Service, Berlin porcelain, about 1819

biscuit porcelain river gods appropriate to his career. The second large case on the south wall contains part of a set of 48 *gros bleu* Sèvres porcelain dessert plates made from 1821 to 1822 and presented to the Duke by King Louis XVIII in 1823, and pieces from the Austrian Service of Vienna porcelain presented by the Emperor Francis I of Austria in 1820.

Of the two projecting cases on the west window wall the larger contains parts of the Deccan Service, which comprised some 125 pieces of silver parcel gilt, made in London in 1805 to 1807 by John Edward; it was presented to the Duke, when Major-General Sir Arthur Wellesley, by officers who had served in the division under his command in the Indian campaigns of 1803. This case also contains a silver centre-piece made by Paul Storr (1771-1844) in 1811 to 1812 and presented to the Duke by the Field Officers of the Peninsular Army. The smaller projecting case contains another Storr centre-piece, dated 1810 to 1811 and presented by the General Officers of the Peninsular Army, and the silver Waterloo Vase of 1824 to 1825, designed by Thomas Stothard and presented to the Duke in 1826 by a group of noblemen and gentlemen, to commemorate the Battle of Waterloo.

Detail of an ice-bucket from the Prussian Service, Berlin porcelain, about 1819

By the window are watercolours by Thomas Shotter Boys (1803-1874) showing the original Plate and China Room in 1852 and 1853. During the refurbishment of the House from 1992-95 the opportunity was taken to reveal two of the windows and restore the decorative scheme of the room which originally occupied the north-west corner of the building. Fibre-optic lighting has been installed in the showcases to provide unobtrusive illumination which is harmless to the collection.

Snuff box, St Petersburg, presented by the Emperor Alexander I of Russia in about 1820

Snuff box, London, 1812, presented with the Freedom of the Borough of Plymouth in 1812

Standard candelabrum made by
Benjamin Smith about 1816

Right: Baton of Field Marshal in the British Army, made by Rundell, Bridge and Rundell and presented by George IV to Wellington in 1821

Above the fireplace is a frame (1981) containing ten of the Duke's batons – British (three, one presented by the Prince Regent in 1813), Portuguese (1809), Hanoverian (1844), Dutch, Spanish (1808), Austrian (1818), and Prussian, together with his staff as High Constable of England (1837 to 1838). Three further wall frames (1981) contain respectively thirteen gold and silver swords and daggers. The most notable among the latter are, on the left, Napoleon's court sword, taken from his carriage after the Battle of Waterloo and later acquired by the Duke, the Duke's own Waterloo sword, a plain example by Napoleon's goldsmith, Biennais, and, on the right, Tippoo Sahib's sword and dagger, said to have been taken from his body after the capture of Seringapatam in 1799. Above the cases hang some of the silver-embroidered French flags presented by Napoleon to the French Departments on the occasion of the assembly known as the *Champ de Mai*, on 1st June 1815.

Baton of Field Marshal of Hanover, by W. Lameyer of Hanover, 1844

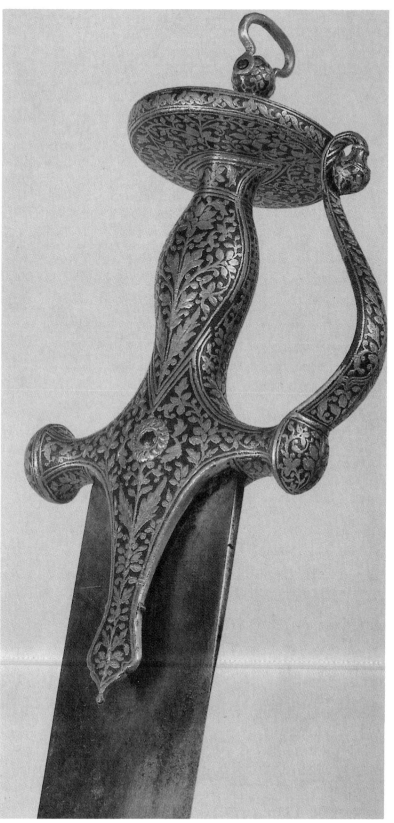

*Right: Hilt of Tippoo Sahib's sword,
Indian (Mysore), about 1790*

*Hilt of Napoléon's court sword, by
Martin Guillaume Biennais, about 1809*

The Basement

The Basement Gallery provides a changing display of plate and china, costume, orders and decorations and other personal effects of the First Duke. Of special note are the costumes worn by the First Duke of Wellington and kindly lent by the present Duke. These include the uniform of an officer in the Grenadier Guards (1827) and of a Marshal General of Portugal (1809); also the robes and regalia of the Order of the Garter (1813) and Chancellor of Oxford (1834).

Amongst the plate are pieces from the Portuguese Service presented to the Duke of Wellington in 1816 by the Portuguese Council of Regency and designed by D.A. de Sequeira (1768-1857) (see p.63). There is also a range of pieces from the Ambassador Service, which consists of some 650 pieces of silver and silver-gilt plate first used by the Duke of Wellington in Paris in 1814 when he was British Ambassador to the Court of France. In contrast, there is also a selection of the Duke's Campaign Plate: simple functional pieces of English, French, Spanish and Portuguese silver used by the First Duke during the Peninsular Campaign 1808-1814.

The porcelain includes a selection from the Saxon Service made in about 1818 by the Meissen factory and presented to the Duke of Wellington by King Frederick Augustus IV of Saxony. Among 105 hand painted dessert plates are two which show Apsley House as built by Robert Adam before it was enlarged by the Duke of Wellington. The remainder have scenes of places relating to the Napoleonic Wars and also of battles fought by the Alliance. There are also pieces from the Austrian Service of Vienna porcelain presented to the Duke by Emperor Francis I of Austria in 1820.

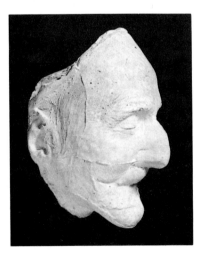

Wellington's Death Mask, taken by George Gamon Adams; plaster, 1852

There are two Déjeuner sets contained within their fitted wooden travel cases. One is of Sèvres porcelain, painted by Langlacé in 1813, awarded a prize in 1815, and presented to the Duke by King Louis XVIII of France. The other was made by the Guérard and Dihl factory in Paris in about 1810 and was taken from the coach of Joseph Bonaparte following his defeat at the Battle of Vitoria in 1813.

The Gallery also displays a selection of the foreign orders conferred on the Duke by the grateful rulers of Europe from 1811 onwards. These include the Military Order of Willem (Netherlands: conferred in 1815), Order of St Januarius (The Two Sicilies: conferred in 1817), Order of the St Esprit (France: conferred in 1815), Grand Cross of the Order of Fidelity (Baden: conferred in 1815), Royal Military Order of Maximilian Joseph (Bavaria: conferred in 1815), Order of the Elephant (Denmark: conferred in 1815), Order of St Alexander Nevsky (Russia: conferred in 1816), Royal Military Order of St Hermenegildo (Spain: conferred in 1816), Royal Military Order of St Ferdinand (Spain: conferred in 1812), Order of the Green Crown (Saxony: conferred in 1815), Imperial Military Order of Maria Theresa (Austria: conferred in 1814), Royal Military Order of St Ferdinand

Plate from the Saxon Service of Meissen porcelain showing Apsley House, about 1818

and of Merit (The Two Sicilies: conferred in 1817), Imperial Military Order of St George (Russia: conferred in 1814), Royal Hanoverian Guelphic Order (Hanover: conferred in 1816), Order of the Black Eagle (Prussia: conferred in 1815), Order of St Andrew (Russia: conferred in 1815), Supreme Order of the Annunziata (Savoy: conferred in 1815), Order of the Red Eagle of Brandenburg (Prussia: conferred in 1815), Order of the Lion (Baden: conferred in 1815), Order of the Crown (Wurttenberg: conferred in 1815), Royal Military Order of the Sword (Sweden: conferred in 1814), English Peninsular Medal, inscribed SALAMANCA, Spanish medal commemorating the restoration of the Spanish monarchy in 1812, Spanish medal commemorating the Battle of Vitoria, 1813, English Peninsular Medal, inscribed Rolica, Vimieiro, Talavera, 1808-9, Order of the Lion d'Or of Hesse Cassel (Hesse Cassel: conferred in 1815), Order of the Golden Fleece (Spain: conferred in 1812).

The Duke's English orders comprise the Order of the Garter (collar, garter and small George: conferred 4 March 1813) and the Order of the Bath (collar: conferred September 1804), together with a Collar of Honour designed by Sir George Nayler and presented by George IV in 1825. There are also the keys of Ciudad Rodrigo and Pamplona, and orders written at Waterloo on prepared slips of vellum, along with the Duke's Peninsular Medal, the only example with all nine clasps, and his own Waterloo Medal, as given to all present at the battle.

Also shown is Wellington's Death Mask taken by the sculptor George Gamon Adams three days after the Duke's death at Walmer Castle in 1852. It was acquired in 1988 with generous assistance from the National Heritage Memorial Fund.

Beyond the Basement Gallery is the Basement Corridor which contains various relics and mementos of the Duke, some of which were presented by the United Services Institution and others collected by the boot blacking firm, John Oakley & Sons (1833-1964) were given by Mr C.A. Oakley. Of special note is a lock of hair from the Duke's chestnut stallion, Copenhagen; a gold bracelet with two attached lockets each containing a lock of the Duke's hair presented by Wellington to his God Daughter, Mary Eleanor Davies Evans, daughter of Charlotte Jones of Pantglas, the famous society beauty much admired by the Duke in his old age.

There are also mementos from the Duchess of Richmond's Ball held in Brussels three days before the Battle of Waterloo, as well as many items relating to the Duke's funeral, (18 November 1852), one of the great spectacles of the nineteenth century.

Throughout the Basement can be seen a changing display from the collection of over 150 works on paper. Among these are political cartoons of the First Duke published by Thomas McLean 1827-1832, including the famous Wellington Boot. Most are by the caricaturist William Heath.

The present arrangement of the Basement is, in the main, a consequence of the Hyde Park road improvement scheme of 1961 to 1962. The part of the Basement not on view and now altered and adapted for staff use, formerly included the Servants Hall and the Kitchen.

The Staircase

Opposite: Napoleon, by Antonio Canova, 1806

The Staircase, dominated by Canova's Napoleon which was placed there in 1817, was further recast by Benjamin Dean Wyatt in about 1830, when the white-and-gold iron balustrade, similar to that at Lancaster House, was installed. Under the First Duke of Wellington there was a flat glass ceiling filled with yellow glass. In about 1860 the Second Duke installed the present dome and the surviving 'sun' gas burner; the chandelier of about 1840 below it is a modern introduction. The ceiling plasterwork with a 'W' and a coronet is original as is the recently restored wall colour, a greenish buff stone. Originally the landing, stairs and lower floor of the Staircase were covered in a patterned carpet, and it is hoped to restore this.
On the landing are full-length portraits of Napoleon, by Robert Lefèvre (1755-1830), King John VI of Portugal, King Frederick William III of Prussia, and King Charles X of France, the latter by Baron Gérard (1770-1837).

Detail of the figure of Victory held by Canova's Napoleon

In 1802 Napoleon summoned the great neo-classical sculptor Antonio Canova (1757-1822) to Paris to model his portrait. Canova then returned to Rome with a plaster model and proceeded to create the full-sized plaster bust now in the Museo Canova at his birthplace, Possagno near Treviso. The Apsley House statue, based on these preparatory works, was completed in about 1810. Its pose was influenced by a statue of a Hellenistic athlete in the Uffizi Gallery in Florence. The statue stands 11 feet 4 inches (3.455 m.) from the feet to the raised left hand. Completed in 1806 it was finally set up in the Louvre on February 6th 1811, for Napoleon to inspect. Nearly nine years had passed since the commission and he did not like the result, saying that it was too athletic and that Canova had failed to express his calm dignity. The statue was packed away in the Louvre until 1816 when it was bought by the British Government for 66,000 francs and presented by King George IV (then Regent) to the Duke of Wellington.

It was packed in a strong case lined with soft cushions, and landed at the Duke of Richmond's Gardens, near Whitehall, where it was placed in an outhouse until its removal to Apsley House on June 1st 1817. According to the *Quarterly Review* Canova 'on learning the final destination of his work, wrote immediately . . . minutely detailing how the statue was to be put up, referring to a mark still to be found on the pedestal, which a plumb line suspended from the right breast would touch'. A full-length bronze replica cast by Righetti in Rome in 1810 is in the courtyard of the Brera Gallery in Milan; it was ordered by Eugène de Beauharnais, Viceroy of Italy. Also in 1810 Righetti executed a small replica, since 1846 in the Louvre.

The Piccadilly Drawing Room

The Piccadilly Drawing Room was designed in 1774 by Robert Adam, whose frieze, doors, ceiling ornament, and marble chimney piece remain, the latter inspired by an engraving by G.B.Piranesi (1720-1778). In 1828 Benjamin Dean Wyatt transformed the room into his 'First Drawing Room', sweeping away the columns and niches in Adam's apse, and introducing the present white and gold colour scheme, restored in 1980. The curtains and wall-hangings are copies of the original 'Yellow Silk Tabaret', the carpet is also a copy of the original, and mirrors have been reintroduced in the pilasters of the apse. The mirror above the chimney piece was not here in 1854, but was present in 1857; it follows a Wyatt design and may well be original to the room. The magnificent chandelier was here in 1854, as were the armchairs, kindly lent by the present Duke of Wellington. In 1854 there was also 'a couch, a corner ottoman, a square ottoman . . . 12 Italian chairs with cane & willow seats . . . a pedestal table, a marble-topped centre table, a sofa-table, 2 card tables, a bookcase with marble top and an Octagon Pianoforte' among other items.

A Musical Party, by Pieter de Hooch, about 1675

Chelsea Pensioners reading the Waterloo Despatch, by Sir David Wilkie, R.A., 1822

The paintings are as follows:

NORTH WALL (left to right)

† *Dutch shipping in a river.*
By Abraham Storck (1644-after 1704).
Signed *A. Storck.*

† *Landscape with classical ruins and figures.*
By Bartholomeus Breenbergh (1598/1600-1657).

Interior with a Cavalier drinking and a couple embracing.
By Willem van Mieris (1662-1747).

★ *Chelsea Pensioners reading the Waterloo despatch.*
By Sir David Wilkie, R.A. (1785-1841).
Signed *David Wilkie, 1822.* Commissioned by the Duke of Wellington
in 1816.

† *An Encampment.*
By Jacques François Joseph Swebach, called Fontaine (or Swebach-
Desfontaines) (1769-1823).
Signed *Swebach dit font* (aine) *1796.*

A Village Scene.
By Jan Victors (1620-about 1676).
Signed *Jan Victors Fect 1654.*

★ *The Greenwich Pensioners commemorating Trafalgar.*
By John Burnet, F.R.S. (1784-1868).
Signed *Jno. B/Oct.21/18* (sic).

A lady at her toilet.
By Caspar Netscher (1635/6-1684).
Signed *G. Netscher f.*

† *The river bank: landscape with figures and cattle.*
By Karel Du Jardin (1621/2-1678).
Signed (?) *K.D.*

† *Self-portrait of an unknown painter.*
Netherlandish School, 1596.

† *A Shipwreck.*
After Claude-Joseph Vernet (1714-1789).

† *Landscape with St Hubert and the stag.*
By Paul Bril (1554-1626).
Signed *PA-- BRIL.*

† *A Harvest Scene.*
By David Teniers the younger (1610-1690).
Signed *D Teniers F.*

EAST WALL (left to right)

† *Landscape with shepherds and a distant view of a castle.*
By David Teniers the younger (1610-1690).

Judith slaying Holofernes, by
Adam Elsheimer, about 1603

† *A lime-kiln with figures.*
By David Teniers the younger (1610-1690).
Signed *D. TENIERS F.*

Landscape with travellers resting.
By Johannes Lingelbach (1622-1674).
Signed *LB* (monogram).

A village merrymaking at a country inn.
By David Teniers the younger (1610-1690).
Signed and dated *D. TENIERS. FIC. 1655.*

† *Landscape with two shepherds, cattle and ducks.*
By David Teniers the younger (1610-1690).
Signed *D. TENIERS F.*

† *Peasants playing bowls in front of an inn by a river.*
By David Teniers the younger (1610-1690).
Signed *D. TENIERS F.*

† *Judith slaying Holofernes.*
By Adam Elsheimer (1578-1610).
Bought from the estate of Rubens by Don Francisco de Rochas for
Philip IV of Spain.

† *The Holy Family with St Elizabeth and St John.*
After Sir Peter Paul Rubens (1577-1640).
17th century copy of a painting by Rubens in the Wallace Collection.

† *The Last Supper, with the institution of the Eucharist and Christ washing
the Disciples' feet.*
Workshop of Juan de Flandes (active 1496; died before 1519).
One of a series of 47 small panels recorded as having belonged to
Queen Isabella of Spain (died 1504).

SOUTH WALL

The rape of Proserpina.
By Jan van Huysum (1682-1749).

† *Camp scene with bugler and farrier's booth.*
By Philips Wouverman (1619-1668).
Signed *PHLS* (monogram) *W.*

*† *Card Players.*
Ascribed to Antiveduto Grammatica (about 1571-1626).
Formerly attributed to Caravaggio.

† *View of the artist's house "De Dry Toren" near Perck.*
By David Teniers the younger (1610-1690).
Signed *D.T.F.* (DT in monogram).

† *The angels guiding the shepherds to the Nativity.*
By Cornelis van Poelenburgh (about 1595-1667).
Signed *C.P.*

† *Landscape with figures crossing a brook.*
By Peeter Gysels (1621-1690/1).
Signed *p. gijsels.*

The intruder: a lady at her toilet, surprised by her lover.
By Pieter de Hooch (1629-after 1684).
Signed *P.D.Hooch.*
Bought by the Duke of Wellington before 1821 (not, as stated elsewhere, captured at Vittoria).

WEST WALL

A warship at anchor in a rough sea.
By Ludolf Bakhuizen (1631-1708).
Signed *L. BAKHUYZEN F.1685.*

The Milkwoman.
By Nicolaes Maes (1634-1693).
Signed *N. MAES.*

★ *The Smokers.*
By Adriaen Brouwer (1606?-1638).
Signed *Braw . . .*

A Flemish village festival.
By David Teniers the younger (1610-1690).
Signed *DAVID TENIERS FC 1639.*
Possibly from the Spanish royal collection; bought for the Duke in 1840.

★ *A musical party.*
By Pieter de Hooch (1629-after 1684).
Signed *P.D.HOO(GE).*

† *Landscape with deer.*
By François van Knibbergen (1597-after 1665).
Signed *F. KNIBBERGEN.*

The Eavesdropper.
By Nicolaes Maes (1634-1693).
Signed *N. MAES. P.*

The physician's visit.
By Jan Steen (1625/6-1679).
Signed *J. Steen.*

The Portico Drawing Room

The Portico Drawing Room originally faced Hyde Park to the West. Robert Adam designed the smaller doors and door-cases, the chimney piece, and the decoration of the ceiling whose frieze incorporates stags suggested by those supporting the Bathurst coat-of-arms. Benjamin Dean Wyatt created the present windows in the south wall under his portico when those to the West had to be closed to allow the addition of the Waterloo Gallery. This is entered through a new door by Wyatt, detailed to match those by Adam, but on a much grander scale. Wyatt replaced the predominantly green Adam colour scheme on walls and ceiling with a white and gold scheme similar to that in the Piccadilly Drawing Room. He also designed the mirror frames and the two side-tables. The Wyatt scheme was restored in 1978, when the curtains were reconstructed and a copy of the original carpet was supplied.

Vase painted with a quagga, Sèvres porcelain, 1814

40

In the 1854 Inventory the Portico Drawing Room was called the 'Large Drawing Room'; its contents included, in addition to the existing side-tables, four more side-tables, a circular and an octagonal pedestal table, two large sofas, seven elbow chairs and twelve 'Italian' chairs. The two great Sèvres porcelain vases on the side tables have always been in the room. Made in 1814, they are painted with, respectively, a quagga and a gnu, animals derived at second hand from aquatints illustrating Samuel Daniell's *African Scenery and Animals,* 1804.

The paintings are as follows:

WEST WALL (left to right)

*   *William Pitt, M.P.* (1759-1806).
    By John Hoppner, R.A. (1758-1810).
    Prime Minister 1783-1801 and 1804-1806.

*   *The illicit Highland whisky still.*
    By Sir Edwin Landseer, R.A. (1802-1873).
    Commissioned by the Duke.

*   *Copy of Raphael's "Madonna with the fish".*
    By Féréol Bonnemaison (active 1796; died 1827).
    The frame is a modern copy of the original frame of the Bonnemaison 'Holy Family' (opposite).
    Given by the Duke of Wellington in 1980.

*   *Marshal Nicolas Jean de Dieu Soult, Duc de Dalmatie* (1769-1852).
    By George Peter Alexander Healy (1808-1894).
    Served under Napoleon in the Peninsular War and at Waterloo.

*   *Spencer Perceval* (1762-1812).
    By George Francis Joseph, A.R.A. (1764-1846).
    Prime Minister 1809 to 1818, when assassinated.

*   *Copy of Raphael's "Christ carrying the Cross".*
    By Féréol Bonnemaison (active 1796; died 1827).
    The frame is a modern copy of the original frame of the Bonnemaison 'Holy Family' (opposite).
    Given by the Duke of Wellington in 1980.

NORTH WALL

*   *Frederick William, Duke of Brunswick* (1771-1815).
    German School, about 1810-15.
    Brother of Queen Caroline; fought with the British Army in the Peninsular War; killed fighting Napoleon at Quatre Bras.

*   *The Rt. Hon. Charles Arbuthnot, M.P.* (1767-1850).
    By Spiridone Gambardella (?1815-1886).
    Dated (on the back) 1849.
    Diplomat and politician.

Chimneypiece of the Portico Drawing Room, designed by Robert Adam, about 1775

'Chimneypiece for the 2d. Drawing room at Apsley House', by Robert Adam, about 1775. Sir John Soane's Museum

EAST WALL

* ★ *Pope Pius VII* (1742-1823).
  By Robert Lefèvre (1755-1830).
  Signed *Robert Lefèvre ft. 1805 à Paris.*

* ★ *Copy of Raphael's "Holy Family", called "La Perla".*
  By Féréol Bonnemaison (active 1796; died 1827).
  Given by the Duke of Wellington in 1980.

* ★ *Napoleon Bonaparte* (1769-1821) as First Consul.
  By Laurent Dabos (1761-1835).

* ★ *The Empress Josephine* (1763-1814).
  By Robert Lefèvre (1755-1830).
  Signed *Robert Lefèvre/ft. 1806.*

* ★ *Copy of Raphael's "Visitation, with the baptism in the distance".*
  By Féréol Bonnemaison (active 1796; died 1827).
  The frame is a modern copy of the original frame of the Bonnemaison "Holy Family" (left of fireplace).

* ★ *The Empress Josephine* (1763-1814).
  By Robert Lefèvre (1755-1830).

  Napoleon Bonaparte (1769-1821).
  After Baron François-Pascal-Simon Gérard (1770-1837).

* ★ *Napoleon in the prison of Nice in 1794.*
  By Edward Matthew Ward, R.A. (1816-1879).
  Signed *EMW 1841.*

The Madonna del Pesce; copy by Féréol Bonnemaison after Raphael, about 1817

Chimney Piece for the 2d Drawing room at Apsley House

43

The Waterloo Gallery

The Waterloo Gallery was designed by Benjamin Dean Wyatt in 1828 for the display of the Duke of Wellington's magnificent collection of paintings, many captured at the Battle of Vitoria in 1813 and subsequently presented to the Duke by King Ferdinand VII of Spain. From 1830 to 1852 the annual Waterloo Banquets were held here; that of 1836 is shown in a print after William Salter, R.A. (1804-1875), displayed on an easel. The Gallery, 90 feet (27.43 metres) long, is in Wyatt's 'Louis XIV' style; the windows are fitted with sliding mirrors which transform it, at night, into an evocation of Louis XIV's Galerie des Glaces at Versailles. The white and gold ceiling incorporates the badge and collar of the Order of the Garter, the Duke's crest, and his coat-of-arms. His friend, Mrs Arbuthnot, claimed to have assisted Wyatt on the design of such ornaments as the gilt cornices above doors and windows. The plasterwork was by the firm of Bernasconi, the other ornaments, of 'paste composition' on a wood base, by George Jackson & Sons. Wyatt also designed the three rococo style chimney pieces, executed in a yellow Siena marble which echoes the gold so prominent in the rest of the Gallery's decorations, and the elaborate parquetry border to the floor.

The Gallery was even more gold under the First Duke because, against the advice of Mrs Arbuthnot and Wyatt, he chose yellow silk damask hangings for the walls. The Second Duke changed this to the present red, but it is hoped to revert to the First Duke's colour, when the paintings will be hung, as in his day, from gilt chains. The furniture comprises a set of English gilt seat furniture, which was probably supplied in about 1760 to the Duke's country house, Stratfield Saye, and which is listed in the Gallery in the 1854 Inventory. There are also two ottomans for public use (1982). The Gallery also contains two great candelabra of grey Siberian porphyry given to the First Duke by the Emperor Nicholas I of Russia, and two vases of Swedish porphyry, on loan from the present Duke, which were presented by King Charles John XIV of Sweden (Marshal Bernadotte); the latter support porcelain candelabra from the Prussian Service (see p.18). The chandelier, English about 1830, has always been at Apsley House, although not always in this room. The carpet (1978) is a copy of the original, as shown in Salter's painting of 1836.

The hanging of the paintings, revised in 1980, reflects the original scheme as recorded in the watercolour by Joseph Nash illustrated here, and in other visual or documentary records. However the First Duke is said to have had about 130 paintings in the Gallery, as opposed to the 70 now present, and his top tier has been necessarily omitted. The positions of the three large paintings above the chimney pieces, the Van Dyck of King Charles I, the Moro of Queen Mary Tudor ('Bloody Mary', as the First Duke called her), and the Hans von Aachen of the Emperor Rudolf II ('Rodolph of

Hapsburgh'), had already been decided before the Gallery was built. They have elaborate frames designed by Wyatt and made by Thomas Temple & Son. By contrast the Goya equestrian portrait of the Duke was disliked by its subject and kept by him in store at Stratfield Saye.

The paintings are as follows:

SOUTH WALL

* *A man of rank embarking at Amsterdam.*
  By Ludolf Bakhuizen (1631-1708).
  Signed *L. Bakhuyzen F.1685.*

* *The Egg Dance: peasants merrymaking in an inn.*
  By Jan Steen (1625/6-1679).

* *The courtyard of an inn with a game of shuffleboard.*
  By Adriaen van Ostade (1610-1685).
  Signed *A v Ostade 1677.*
  Formerly in the collection of the Duc de Choiseul.

* *The Emperor Rudolf II (1552-1612).*
  By Hans von Aachen (1552-1615).

† *River scene with boats and figures.*
  By Jan Brueghel I (1568-1625).
  Signed *BRVEGHEL 16(?06).*

† *Entering the Ark.*
By Jan Brueghel I (1568-1625).
Signed *BRVEGHEL 1615.*

★† *Large ships and boats in a calm.*
By Willem van de Velde the younger (1633-1707).
Signed *WVV.*

† *Venus and Adonis.*
Ascribed to Carlo Cignani (1628-1719).

★ *A Wedding Party.*
By Jan Steen (1625/6-1679).
Signed *J. Steen 1667.*

WEST WALL

† *Virgin and Child.*
Italian School, about 1600.

† *The Virgin and Child with St Carlo Borromeo.*
Ascribed to Francesco Trevisani (1656-1746).

† *The Expulsion from Paradise.*
By Giuseppe Cesari, called Il Cavaliere d'Arpino (1568-1640).

† *Saint Catherine of Alexandria.*
By Claudio Coello (1642-1693).
Inscribed *CLAUD. COELL. FA. PICT. REG. ANNO 1683.*

★† *The departure of a hawking party.*
By Philips Wouverman (1619-1668).
Signed *P.H.* (monogram) *W.*

† *The Holy Family with the Infant St John.*
By a follower of Bernardino Luini (active 1512; died 1532).

Architectural fantasy, with the Old Town Hall, Amsterdam.
By Jan van der Heyden (1637-1712).
Signed *V. Heyde f.*

Landscape with the Flight into Egypt.
Traditionally ascribed to Sir Joshua Reynolds, P.R.A. (1723-1792).

★† *The Annunciation.*
By Marcello Venusti (1512/15-1579).

★† *An unknown lady, called "Titian's mistress".*
By a follower of Titian (Tiziano Vercellio) (about 1482-1576).

★† *La Carcasse: a witch being drawn on the skeleton of a monster.*
Traditionally ascribed to Jusepe de Ribera, called Lo Spagnoletto
(1591-1652).

Portrait of a man.
Italian School.

*The Agony in the Garden, by Antonio
Allegri, called Correggio, about 1525*

Saint Rosalie, by Sir Anthony Van Dyck, 1624

Ana Dorotea, daughter of Rudolf II, by Sir Peter Paul Rubens, 1628

50

Head of St Joseph.
By Guido Reni (1575-1642).
From the Spanish Royal Collection; presented to the Duke by the Intendant of Segovia in 1812.

† *Head of an old man.*
By Sir Peter Paul Rubens (1577-1640).

A sainted nun.
Italian School, 16th century.
From the Spanish Royal Collection; presented to the Duke by the Intendant of Segovia in 1812.

★ *The Château of Goudestein*, on the River Vecht, near Maarsen.
By Jan van der Heyden (1637-1712).
Signed *J.V.D. Heyde/1674.*

A musical party.
By Willem Cornelisz Duyster (c.1599-1625).
Signed W.C.D.A. 1634.

† *The Virgin and Child with St Elizabeth and the infant St John.*
By Giovanni Battista Salvi, called Sassoferrato (1609-1685).

★† *The return from the chase.*
By Philips Wouverman (1619-1668).
Signed *PH* (monogram) *W.*

NORTH WALL

An unknown lady.
Venetian School, 16th century.

★ *Mars as a warrior.*
By Guercino (1591-1666).

★† *The Virgin and Child.*
By Giulio Romano (1492 or 1499-1546).

★† *Virgin and Child.*
By Giovanni Battista Salvi, called Sassoferrato (1609-1685).

★ *Queen Mary I of England* (1516-1558).
After Anthonis Mor (Antonio Moro) (about 1519-1576/7).

† *Travellers on a country road, with cattle and pigs.*
By Jan Brueghel I (1568-1625).
Signed *BRVEGHEL. 1616.*

Road scene with travellers and cattle.
By Jan Brueghel I (1568-1625).

† *Country road scene with figures: a man praying at a shrine.*
By Jan Brueghel I (1568-1625).

Doge Marcantonio Memmo(1536-1615).
Ascribed to Leandro Bassano (1557-1622).

Venus and Cupid.
By Guercino (1591-1666).

★ *The Mystic Marriage of St Catherine.*
By Giuseppe Cesari, called Il Cavaliere d'Arpino (1568-1640).

★† *The Agony in the Garden.*
By Antonio Allegri, called Correggio (about 1494-1534).
Praised by Vasari (1568); the Duke's favourite painting.

EAST WALL

★ *The entry of Philip IV into Pamplona.*
By Juan Bautista del Mazo (about 1612/16-1667).

† *River view: evening.*
By Aert van der Neer (1603/04-1677).
Signed *AV DN* (two monograms).

★† *Pope Innocent X.*
Ascribed to Diego Velazquez (1599-1660).

★† *The Holy Family with the Infant St John.*
By Anton Raphael Mengs (1728-1779).
Signed *ANTONIUS. RAPHAEL. MENGS. SAX. FACEB. MDCCLXV.*

★† *Battle scene with classical colonnade.*
By Salvator Rosa (1615-1673).
Signed *SR* (monogram).

★† *Interior of a cowshed.*
By David Teniers the younger (1610-1690).

★† *Two young men eating at a humble table.*
By Diego Velazquez (1599-1599).

★† *A Spanish gentleman, probably José Nieto, Chamberlain to Queen Mariana of Austria, wife of Philip IV.*
By Diego Velazquez (1559-1599).

† *Hercules wrestling with Achelous in the form of a bull.*
After Sir Peter Paul Rubens (1577-1640).
Companion piece to *Hercules and the Nemean lion* (to the right).

★† *The Infant Christ appearing to St Anthony of Padua.*
By Anton Raphael Mengs (1728-1779).

★ *Francisco Gomes de Quevedo y Villegas* (1580-1645).
Studio of Diego Velazquez (1599-1660).

A Musician.
By Cecco del Caravaggio (active c.1600-1620).
Traditionally known as *The Conjuror.*

★† *The Waterseller of Seville.*
By Diego Velazquez (1599-1660).
The most famous of the *bodegones* painted by Velazquez in Seville in about 1620.

Hercules and the Nemean lion.
After Sir Peter Paul Rubens (1577-1640).

Companion piece to *Hercules wrestling with Achelous in the form of a bull* (to the left).

★ *The Crucifixion, with the fall of the rebel angels.*
By Cornelius van Poelenburgh (about 1595-1667).
Signed *C.P.*

★ *St James the Great.*
By Jusepe de Ribera, called Lo Spagnoletto (1591-1652).

★ *Charles I (1600-1649) on horseback with M. de St Antonie.*
After Sir Anthony van Dyck (1599-1641).
The original, painted for St James's Palace in 1633, now at Buckingham Palace.

★† *The Mystic Marriage of St Catherine.*
After Parmigianino (1503-1540).

St Rosalie crowned with roses by two angels.
By Sir Anthony van Dyck (1599-1641).

★ *St Francis receiving the stigmata.*
By Bartolomé Esteban Murillo (1617-1682).

★ *Orpheus enchanting the animals.*
Ascribed to Alessandro Varotari, Il Padovanino (1588-1648).

An unknown man.
Ascribed to Bartolomé Esteban Murillo (1617-1682).

★ *The Virgin with the standing Child.*
Ascribed to Bernardino Luini (active 1512; died 1532).
A replica of Luini's *Virgin of the Columbine* in the Wallace Collection.

Ana Dorotea, Daughter of Rudolf II, a nun at the Convent of the Descalzas Reales, Madrid.
By Sir Peter Paul Rubens (1577-1640).

St John the Baptist.
By Jusepe de Ribera, called Lo Spagnoletto (1591-1652).
Signed *Jusepe de Ribera/espanol/F.1650.*

★ *The Colbert family.*
By Adam François van der Meulen (1632-1690).

French generals arriving before a town.
By Adam François van der Meulen (1632-1690).
Signed *F.V. MEULEN 1678.*

Louis XIV at a siege.
By Adam François van der Meulen (1632-1690).

★ *The Dissolute Household.*
By Jan Steen (1625/6-1679).
Signed *J. Steen.*

Equestrian portrait of the Duke of Wellington.
By Francisco de Goya (1746-1828).

The Yellow Drawing Room

The Yellow Drawing Room, called the Small Drawing Room in 1854 and the North West Drawing Room in 1857, occupies the site of Robert Adam's Third Drawing Room; only his doorcases to the Portico Drawing Room remain.
The two large doorcases were designed by Benjamin Dean Wyatt, together with the white marble chimney piece and the cornice with its paired gilt consoles. The chandelier is English, about 1830. The two tables, with red porphyry tops supported on lion monopodia, are French about 1810. That by the window supports a delicate marble bust by Antonio Canova (1757-1822) of a dancer. This was given by Canova to Wellington in 1817, in recompense for his efforts to restore to Rome art treasures taken by the French to Paris. In 1854 the room also contained a Grecian couch, ten chairs, a writing-table and two other tables, a small cabinet and five stands.

The paintings are as follows:

WEST WALL
> *Landscape with peasants driving cattle: evening.*
> David Teniers the younger (1610-1690).
> Signed *D. TENIERS FEC.*

> *St Paul at Malta, grasping the viper.*
> By Giovanni Paolo Panini (or Pannini) (1691/2-1765?).
> Signed *I.P.P. 1735.*
> Companion piece to *St Paul at Athens.*

A festival in the Piazza di Spagna, Rome, by Giovanni Paolo Panini, 1727

The Death of Cleopatra.
By Johann Georg Platzer (1704-1761).

★ *King William IV* (1765-1837).
By Sir David Wilkie, R.A. (1785-1841).
Signed *David Wilkie f. Brighton 1833.*
Presented to the Duke of Wellington by William IV in 1833.

† *Landscape with bleaching grounds.*
By a follower of Jacob van Ruisdael (1628/9-1682).
Indistinctly signed (?) *Gi... or Ri... .*
Traditionally attributed to Jan Vermeer van Haarlem (1628-1691).

St Paul preaching at Athens.
By Giovanni Paolo Panini (or Pannini) (1691/2-1765?).
Signed *I.P.P. 1737.*
Companion piece to *St Paul at Malta.*

Anthony and Cleopatra at the Battle of Actium.
By Johann Georg Platzer (1704-1761).

SOUTH WALL

Samson and Delilah (Judges XVI, 19).
By Luca Giordino (1634-1705).

Self-portrait, wearing glasses.
After Sir Joshua Reynolds, P.R.A. (1723-1792).
Contemporary copy of the self-portrait, painted in 1788, in the Royal
Collection at Windsor Castle.

Sunset: view over a bay with figures.
By Claude-Joseph Vernet (1714-1789).
Painted in 1742.

A festival in the Piazza di Spagna, Rome, 1727.
By Giovanni Paolo Panini (or Pannini) (1691/2-1765?).
Signed: *I.P. Panini Placentus Romae 1727.*

Hagar and Ishmael in the Desert (Genesis XVI, 7).
By Luca Giordano (1634-1705).

EAST WALL

† *An encampment with soldiers playing cards.*
By Lambert de Hondt (d. before 1665).
Signed *L.D. Hondt. F.*

A Flemish Village with river view.
By Peeter Gysels (1621-1690/1).
Signed *Petrus Geysels.*

Boys with a trapped bird.
By Aert van der Neer (1603/4-1677).
Signed *E. Van der Neer.*

King William IV, by Sir David Wilkie,
R.A., 1833

★ *Richard, Marquess Wellesley, K.C. (1760-1842).*
By C. Fortescue Bates after Sir Martin Archer Shee (1769-1850).
Lent by His Grace the Duke of Wellington.

A Cavalier with a grey horse.
By Abraham van Calraet (1642-1722).
Signed *AC.*

A Flemish Village: the river landing stage.
By Peeter Gysels (1621-1690/1).
Signed *p. gÿsels.* (sic)

Two wings of a triptych: The Virgin and the Angel of Annunciation.
By Marcellus Coffermans (active 1549-1578).

Shepherd and cattle.
By Philipp Peter Ross, called Rosa da Tivoli (1655/7-1706).

Isaac blessing Jacob (Genesis XXVII, 18-29).
By Bartolomé Esteban Murillo (1617-1682).

The Striped Drawing Room, watercolour by Thomas Shotter Boys, 1852

Pastoral Landscape with the Ponte Molle, Rome.
Ascribed to Claude Gelée, called Le Lorrain (1600-82).

The Striped Drawing Room

The Striped Drawing Room, called by the name in 1854 and the North Drawing Room adjoining Dining Room in 1857, was created by Benjamin Dean Wyatt in about 1828 from Robert Adam's bedroom and Etruscan dressing-room of the 1770s. The ceiling, cornice, frieze and chimney piece were all designed by Wyatt. The English cut-glass chandelier dates from about 1830. The two ormolu and malachite side tables and the malachite centre table were given to the Duke of Wellington by Emperor Nicholas of Russia. Above the chimney piece hangs a silk French tricolor standard lent by Her Majesty the Queen. A similar standard is presented to the Sovereign by the Dukes of Wellington on each anniversary of the Battle of Waterloo. They are kept in the Waterloo Chamber at Windsor Castle.

A watercolour of 1853 on display in the room shows it hung with what the 1854 Inventory calls 'rose coloured striped taboret', similar to that now present, the ottomans round the walls with upholstery and valances in the same material, and the same carpet as elsewhere at Apsley House. In his 1853 *Apsley House and Walmer Castle* Richard Ford called this room the 'Walhalla' and noted the presence of many portraits of the Duke's 'comrades of his arms'. There seems little doubt that the striped taboret and ottomans were intended to reinforce this martial theme, producing the effect of a striped military tent, an echo of a famous tent room in Napoleon's apartment at Malmaison, designed by Percier and Fontaine. On the side tables are busts of the Prime Ministers Spencer Perceval (1762-1812) and William Pitt (1759-1806), both by Joseph Nollekens (1737-1823). In 1854 the room also contained a central ottoman, a large sofa...a writing-table, a loo table and an Ecarté table.

The Battle of Waterloo, 1815, by Sir William Allan, 1843

The paintings are as follows:

WEST WALL

★ *Colonel John Gurwood, C.B.* (1790-1845).
By James Hall (1797-1854). Dated 1837.
Private secretary to the Duke of Wellington; edited the *Wellington Despatches*; wounded at Waterloo.

★ *Stapleton Cotton, Field-Marshal Viscount Combermere, G.C.B., K.S.T.,* (1773-1865).
By John Hayter (1800-c.1891). Signed and dated 1839.
Served in India and in the Peninsular War; second in command under Wellington at Salamanca.

★ *Horatio, Viscount Nelson* (1758-1805).
After Sir William Beechey, R.A. (1753-1839).

★ *The Battle of Waterloo.*
By Sir William Allan (1782-1850).
Signed *William Allan Pinxt, 1843.*
This shows the battle from the French side, at 7.30 p.m. on 18 June 1815. It represents "the last desperate effort of Napoleon (seen on the right) to force the left centre of the allied army and turn their position". In the centre are

the advancing battalions of the Imperial Guard, led by Marshall Ney, which are being successfully attacked on three sides by the British. The Duke of Wellington can be seen on the rising ground to the left. He is said to have commented of this painting, 'Good – very good; not too much smoke'.

Field Marshal August Neidhardt, Count of Gneisenau (1760-1831).
By George Dawe, R.A. (1781-1829).
Prussian soldier; served under General Blücher against Napoleon.

★ *Major-General John Fremantle, C.B.* (died 1845).
By Jan Willem Pieneman (1779-1853).
Signed *JWP / Apsly House / London / 1821.*
Served in the Peninsular War and at Waterloo; commanded the British troops in the Crimea.

Field Marshal Lord Fitzroy James Henry Somerset, 1st Baron Raglan, G.C.B. (1788-1855).
By Jan Willem Pieneman (1779-1853).
Signed *JWP / Apsly House / London / 1821.*
Served in the Peninsular War and at Waterloo; commanded the British troops in the Crimea.

SOUTH WALL

- ★ *William II, King of Holland* (1792-1849), when Prince of Orange.
  By John Singleton Copley, R.A. (1737-1815).

- ★ *Lt.-General Sir Thomas Picton, G.C.B.* (1758-1815).
  By Sir William Beechey R.A. (1753-1839).
  Served in the Peninsular War and at Waterloo, where he was killed.

  General Sir George Cooke, K.C.B. (1768-1837).
  By Jan Willem Pieneman (1779-1853). Signed *JWP/Apsly House/London/1821.*
  Served in the Peninsular War, at Quatre Bras and Waterloo.

- ★ *Field Marshal Sir John Colborne, 1st Baron Seaton, G.C.B., G.C.H.* (1778-1863).
  By Jan Willem Pieneman (1779-1853). Signed *JWP/Apsly House/London/1821.*
  Served in the Peninsular War; played a major part in the defeat of
  Napoleon's Old Guard at Waterloo.

- ★ *Thomas Graham, Lord Lynedoch, G.C.B, G.C.M.G.* (1748-1843).
  By Sir Thomas Lawrence, P.R.A. (1769-1830).

  General Sir James Shaw Kennedy, K.C.B. (1788-1865).
  By Jan Willem Pieneman (1779-1853).
  Signed *JWP / Apsly House / London / 1821.*
  Served in the Peninsular War and at Quatre Bras and Waterloo.

- ★ *Field Marshal Prince von Blücher* (1742-1819).
  By George Dawe, R.A. (1781-1829).
  Commander of the Prussian Army.

- ★ *William Pitt* (1759-1806).
  By Gainsborough Dupont (1754-1797).
  Prime Minister 1783-1801 and 1804-1806.

- ★ *William Carr, Viscount Beresford, G.C.B.* (1768-1854).
  By Sir Thomas Lawrence, P.R.A. (1769-1830).
  Served in the Peninsular War as commander of the Portuguese army.

- ★ *Frederick Augustus Duke of York and Albany, K.G.* (1763-1827).
  By Henry Wyatt (1794-1840).
  Commanded British forces in Flanders 1793-5.

- ★ *General Miguel Ricardo de Alava* (1771-1843).
  By George Dawe, R.A. (1781-1829). Signed and dated 1818.
  Spanish officer attached to Wellington's staff in the Peninsular War and
  Waterloo. Later ambassador to England.

  Pauline Bonaparte, Princess Borghese (1780-1825).
  By Robert Lefèvre (1755-1830).
  Signed *Robert Lefèvre ft. 1806.*
  Sister of Napoleon; married, first General Leclerc, later Prince Borghese.

- ★ *Lt.-General Sir Edward Barnes, G.C.B.* (1776-1838).
  By George Dawe, R.A. (1781-1829).
  Served in the Peninsular War and at Waterloo.

- ★ *General Sir George Murray G.C.B.* (1772-1846).
  By John Prescott Knight (1803-1881).
  Served in the Peninsular War; later Master-General of the Ordnance 1834-46.

The First Marquess of Anglesey, K.G., by
Sir Thomas Lawrence, P.R.A., 1818

EAST WALL

★ *General Rowland Hill, Viscount Hill, G.C.B., G.C.H* (1772-1842).
By Jan Willem Pieneman (1779-1853).
Signed *JWP/Apsly (sic) House/London/1821.*
Served in the Peninsular War and at Waterloo; in 1828 appointed
Commander-in-Chief of the army.

★ *General Miguel Ricardo de Alava* (1771-1843).
By Jan Willem Pieneman (1779-1853). Signed *JWP/Apsly House/London/1821.*
Spanish soldier and diplomat; served under the Duke in the Peninsular War
and at Waterloo.

Arthur Wellesley, 1st Duke of Wellington (1769-1852).
By Sir Thomas Lawrence, P.R.A. (1769-1830).
Painted about 1815.

★ *Henry William Paget, 1st Marquess of Anglesey, K.G.* (1768-1854).
By Sir Thomas Lawrence, P.R.A. (1769-1830).
Served at Waterloo; later, Master General of the Ordnance and Lord
Lieutenant of Ireland.

The Duke of Wellington looking at a bust of Napoleon.
By Charles Robert Leslie, R.A. (1794-1859).

★ *Major-General Sir Henry Willoughby Rooke, C.B., K.C.H.* (1782-1869).
By John Hoppner, R.A. (1758-1810).

Henry William Paget, 1st Marquess of Anglesey, K.G. (1768-1854).
By Jan Willem Pieneman (1779-1853). Signed *JWP/Apsly House/London/1821.*
(See above)

Lieut.-Colonel William Thornhill (died 1850).
By Jan Willem Pieneman (1779-1853). Signed *JWP/Apsly House/London/1821.*
Served in the Peninsular War and at Waterloo.

NORTH WALL

Major-General Sir Frederick Cavendish Ponsonby, K.C.B. (1783-1837)
and *Major-General Sir Colin Campbell, K.C.B., K.C.H.* (1776-1847) (left).
By Jan Willem Pieneman (1779-1853). Signed *JWP/Apsly House/London/1821.*
Both officers served in the Peninsular War and at Waterloo.

★ *General Lord Edward Somerset, K.C.B.* (1776-1842).
By Jan Willem Pieneman (1779-1853). Signed *JWP/Apsly House/London/1821.*
Served in the Peninsular War; commanded the household cavalry at Waterloo.

★ *Lieut-General Sir John Elley, K.C.B., K.C.H.* (died 1839).
By Jan Willem Pieneman (1779-1853). Signed *JWP/Apsly House/London/1821.*
Served in the Peninsular War and at Waterloo.

★ *General Sir Colin Halkett, G.C.B., G.C.H.* (1774-1856).
By Jan Willem Pieneman (1779-1853). Signed *JWP/Apsly House/London/1821.*
Served in the Peninsular War and at Waterloo.

The Dining Room

The Dining Room was created by Benjamin Dean Wyatt in 1819. Approached through a mirrored lobby (called the 'Octagon Passage' by Wyatt in 1829), it has a masculine classical interior with buff walls, oak doors, dado, sideboard, plate-warmer and chairs, and an oak-grained cornice supported by massive Corinthian pilasters of Siena scagliola, with gilt bases and capitals. The sideboard, probably supplied by Messrs. Dowbiggin, incorporates a central support for the Wellington Shield (see p.17), which was displayed here at Waterloo Banquets up to 1829. The present carpet and red wool curtains were supplied in 1982. The cut-glass chandelier is English, about 1830.

On the mahogany table stands the 26 feet (7.92 metres) long centrepiece of the Portuguese Service. The complete Service, of silver and silver-gilt, originally consisted of some thousand pieces. It was presented to the Duke of Wellington in 1816 by the Portuguese Council of Regency. Designed by

The Dining Room, watercolour by Thomas Shotter Boys, 1852

63

The Dining Room

King George IV, by Sir David Wilkie, R.A., 1830

D.A. de Sequeira (1768-1857) and made in the Military Arsenal at Lisbon from 1812 to 1816, it is the single great monument of Portuguese neo-classical silver. The central ornament of the centrepiece shows the Four Continents paying tribute to the united armies of Britain, Portugal and Spain. The dancing figures which surround the plateau were originally linked by garlands of silk flowers.

The paintings, since 1982 all in their original positions, are as follows:

WEST WALL

* *Louis XVIII, King of France* (1755-1824).
  By Baron François-Pascal-Simon Gérard (1770-1837).
  Presented to the Duke of Wellington by Charles X in 1826.

* *Francis II, Emperor of Austria* (1768-1835).
  By Anton Einsle (1801-1871).
  Signed *Anton Einsle K.K.* (Kaiserlich Koniglicher) *Hofmaker in Wien 1841.*
  Given to the Duke of Wellington by Ferdinand, Emperor of Austria, in 1842.

EAST WALL

* *Frederick William III, King of Prussia* (1770-1840).
  By Wilhelm Herbig (1787-1861).
  Signed *Herbig pint.*
  Given to the Duke of Wellington by the King of Prussia in 1818.

* *King George IV* (1762-1830).
  By Sir David Wilkie, R.A. (1785-1841).
  Signed *David Wilkie 1830.*
  The Highland dress was worn by the King on his visit to Edinburgh in 1822.

* *Alexander I, Emperor of Russia* (1777-1825).
  By Baron François-Pascal-Simon Gérard (1770-1837).
  Presented to the Duke of Wellington by Alexander I of Russia in 1817.

SOUTH WALL

* *William I, King of Holland* (1772-1843).
  By François Joseph Navez (1787-1869).
  Signed *F.J. Navez, 1823.*
  Presented to the Duke of Wellington by William I of Holland in 1824.

The central feature of the centrepiece of the Portuguese Service, silver parcel gilt, Lisbon, about 1816

The Rest of the House

The rest of Apsley House, apart from certain parts of the Basement used for administrative purposes, was reserved under the Wellington Museum Act of 1947 for the use of the Seventh Duke of Wellington and his successors who are, happily, still in occupation. Certain changes in function and decoration have taken place in some of these private rooms, particularly under the Second Duke of Wellington, but the appearance of the First Duke's own rooms was recorded in the illustrations to Richard Ford's *Apsley House and Walmer Castle*, 1853, reproduced here.

'The Duke's Bed Room', after Thomas Shotter Boys, from Richard Ford, 'Apsley House and Walmer Castle', 1853

'The Duke's own Room', after Thomas
Shotter Boys, from Richard Ford, 'Apsley
House and Walmer Castle', 1853

'The Secretary's Room', after Thomas
Shotter Boys, from Richard Ford, 'Apsley
House and Walmer Castle', 1853

67

Life of the Duke of Wellington
1769-1852

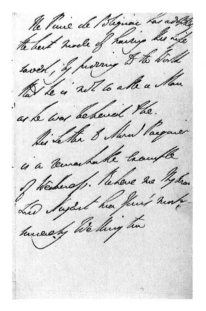

The future Duke of Wellington was born at 24 Upper Merion Street, Dublin, on 29 April (or 1 May?) 1769. He was Arthur Wellesley, the fourth son of Garret Wellesley (or Wesley), first Earl of Mornington, and his wife Anne, the eldest daughter of Viscount Dungannon. Just over three months later Napoleon Bonaparte was born at Ajaccio in Corsica, on 15 August.

Wellington was educated first at Brown's preparatory school in Chelsea, and then at Eton from 1781 to 1784. His father died in 1781 and three years later his mother removed him from Eton and took him to Brussels, where his education was continued privately with Louis Goubert, a barrister.

Early impressions of the boy show him as aloof and rather aggressive, with talents for mathematics and music — he played the violin when young — but otherwise "not very attentive to his studies". His mother decided that the best thing for him was the army, although his constitution was not too robust.

This severe but practical woman remarked that her "ugly boy Arthur" was "fit food for powder". So in 1786 he went to Pignerolle's military academy at Angers in France where he stayed a year. His brief stay there brought him new friends, the devotion of a "little terrier called Vic" and a useful fluency in French.

In 1787 his brother, Lord Mornington, obtained a commission for him in the 73rd (Highland) Regiment — he was gazetted Ensign on 7 March — and then, after the fashion of the time he advanced through five different regiments and became Lieutenant (1787) and Captain (1791). On 30 April 1793, he purchased the commission of major in the 33rd Foot (now the Duke of Wellington's Regiment) and on 30 September of the same year the

Lieutenant-Colonelcy of the regiment. He sailed with it for the Continent in June 1794 to join the Allied armies behind the River Dyle in Belgium.

It was at Boxtel, near Bois-le-Duc in Holland, that Wellesley first saw action, when he distinguished himself by halting a French force which was driving back the Allies. He fought through the months of retreat to the mouth of the Weser (assuming the command of a brigade) where the army embarked for England in the spring of 1795.

During this early period (1787-95) he saw little military service in the strict sense, as he was Aide-de-Camp to two Lords Lieutenant of Ireland, and represented the Irish constituency of Trim in Parliament from 1790 to 1795.

After other minor adventures, he went to India in 1796, being now a Colonel. He had persuaded his eldest brother, Lord Mornington (afterwards Marquess Wellesley) to take the Governor-Generalship of India, and acted as his unofficial adviser. India was to be his true training ground, both as a soldier and a statesman; for he had now decided to take his military career seriously, working strenuously to train himself in all branches of military science. He gave up card-playing and even music — he had burnt his violin in 1793 — in order to devote himself to his work.

In 1799 Wellesley took part in the invasion of Mysore against Tippoo Sultan and was appointed Governor of Seringapatam when it was captured, later being put in charge of the civil administration of Mysore State. He next fought and defeated Dhoondiah, a freebooter who invaded the territory with a large army (1800). After being prevented by illness from going as second in command of the expedition to Egypt — an illness which saved his life, because the troopship was sunk with all hands in the Red Sea — he continued to administer Mysore, during which time he was promoted to Major-General (1802).

When hostilities broke out against the Mahratta tribes (1803), Wellesley took a leading part in the war and inflicted severe defeats on the enemy at Assaye, Argaum and Gawilghur, and afterwards negotiated the treaties which saw the end of the campaign. He received the thanks of Parliament, and the people of Calcutta presented him with a sword of honour. He was now anxious to return to England; "I think I have served as long in India as any man ought who can serve anywhere else", he said. It was during this formative period of life in India that he grew to be an outstanding soldier and a shrewd statesman; his experience had been wide and varied, and he had mastered every department of civil and military administration, as well as proving himself an excellent field commander.

After further minor actions in India, and after declining command of the Bombay army, he resigned his appointments, civil and military (24 February 1805) and sailed for England, where he arrived on 10 September.

After his return to England he commanded a brigade in Lord Cathcart's expedition to Hanover, which returned after Napoleon's victory at Austerlitz (1805); was made Colonel of the 33rd Foot; was given a brigade at Hastings; was re-elected to Parliament (1806) and made Irish Secretary; went to Denmark in 1807 and took part in the surrender of Copenhagen; and was promoted Lieutenant-General on 25 April 1808, the year of commencement of the Peninsular War. He was married 10 April 1806 to the Hon. Catherine Pakenham, second daughter of Edward, second Baron Longford. She died 24 April 1831, in London, and is buried at Stratfield Saye.

A selection of the Campaign Plate

In July 1808 he sailed for Portugal in command of a force of some 9,000 men to assist the Portuguese and Spaniards against the French, and was joined later by reinforcements both from England and from the Portuguese themselves. After winning the Battles of Roliça and Vimieiro, he was made the scapegoat for the unpopular Convention of Cintra, and returned to England on 6 October 1808. Sir John Moore was then appointed to command the army in Portugal. After Moore's glorious death at Corunna (1809) Wellesley was re-appointed to the Command and arrived in Mondego Bay, Portugal, in April 1809.

Wellesley's first successes in the Peninsula were the forcing of the passage of the Douro, and the defeat of Soult's army at Oporto (12 May 1809). He then crossed the Spanish border and, with the help of the Spanish army, again beat the French at Talavera (27-28 June). For these victories he was raised to the peerage and took the titles of Baron Douro of Wellesley and Viscount Wellington of Talavera, this title being chosen by his brother William because Wellington is near Wellesley in Somerset, from which the family originally took its name.

Masséna was appointed by Napoleon to command the French, now reinforced, in the Peninsula. With the arrival of these new French forces, Wellington was forced to withdraw and finally took up positions on the lines of Torres Vedras, outside Lisbon, after defeating Masséna at the Battle of Busaco (27 September 1810).

But Masséna, finding the lines too strong to attack, and running short of supplies, was forced to fall back, followed and harried by Wellington. Actions were fought at Pombal, Redinha, Cazal Nova, Foz d'Aronce and Sabugal (3 April 1811) — this last signalling the end of the French

invasion of Portugal and the retreat of their armies to Salamanca. Wellington now received the confidence and thanks of Parliament and prepared to drive the enemy out of the whole Peninsula. He went over to the offensive, and defeated the French at Fuentes de Onoro, Almeida and Albuera (16 May 1811); but the siege of Badajoz in June was unsuccessful and was raised by the French generals Marmont and Soult. Having once failed to take Ciudad Rodrigo, Wellington again attacked the city and by a brilliant action captured it on 19 January 1812 — an achievement for which he was made an earl and received the acclaim of his own country and of Spain, the latter making him Duke of Ciudad Rodrigo.

The next objective was Badajoz which, at severe cost in lives, was besieged and captured on 6 April 1812. Three months later Wellington defeated Marmont at the Battle of Salamanca (22 July) — "this battle was Wellington's masterpiece" as one writer said — and then went on to occupy Valladolid. On 12 August he entered Madrid. He next marched northwards, but failed to capture Burgos after a month's siege (October) and later fell back to the Portuguese frontier, where the allied armies, British, Spanish, and Portuguese, were brought together in preparation for the campaign of 1813.

Honours were now heaped upon Wellington, of which the most important were his elevation to Marquess (August 1812) with a grant of £100,000 from Parliament; the award of the Order of the Garter (March 1813); and his appointment as generalissimo of the Spanish armies (September 1812).

He opened the campaign of 1813 by advancing into Spain in two columns, one by the north bank of the Douro, the other to Salamanca. The columns pressed forward and joined forces at Toro on 4 June, and advanced upon

Burgos, which the French then abandoned. On 21 June was fought the great Battle of Vitoria in which the French lost about five thousand men, together with most of their guns, stores and loot. Joseph Bonaparte's baggage train, captured with the rest, contained many works of art stolen from the Spaniards, which King Ferdinand afterwards presented to Wellington (see p. 83). For this victory he was promoted to Field Marshal, and received from Spain the estate of Soto de Roma, near Granada.

The French army retreated across the Pyrénées — after continuous and heavy fighting during July and August 1813 — and soon they only had the armies of Aragon and Catalonia left in Spain, with garrisons in Pamplona and San Sebastian, which were blockaded and besieged by the Allies. San Sebastian was finally stormed, and surrendered (9 September); and Pamplona gave in a few weeks later (31 October).

With the war in Germany now settled by the defeat of Napoleon at Leipzig (16-19 October 1813), Wellington advanced into France, driving the French back to Bayonne after the Battles of the Nivelle (16 November) and Nive (9-13 December). Leaving two divisions to blockade Bayonne, Wellington pursued Marshal Soult with the rest of the allied armies. There followed the Battle of Orthez (27 February 1814) and, after lesser actions, the Battle of Toulouse (10 April). Two days later Wellington heard that Napoleon had abdicated; and the convention by which hostilities came to an end was signed on 18 April 1814. After being summoned to Paris, Wellington visited King Ferdinand at Madrid and then returned to England, landing there on 23 May. His home-coming was a triumphal procession, and amidst a fresh shower of honours he was created Marquess Douro and Duke of Wellington, with an extra grant from Parliament of £400,000.

He was, strangely enough, appointed Ambassador to France (5 July 1814), and after much controversy left in February of 1815 to take Lord Castlereagh's place at the Congress of Vienna. But Napoleon returned to France from the Island of Elba on 1 March, and Europe was again in a turmoil. Wellington was appointed Commander of the Anglo-Netherland and Hanoverian forces in Europe (28 March) and by early June held, with Blücher's Prussians, a ninety-mile front just behind the Belgian frontier. Napoleon, with his Grand Army, hoped to drive a wedge between Wellington and Blücher and deal with them piecemeal before help could arrive from the Austrians and Russians. The French attacked on 16 June, defeating the Prussians on the right flank but being beaten at Quatre Bras on the left. Wellington then pulled his forces back at Waterloo to which Blücher promised to send two corps, and there the great battle was fought. On 18 June Napoleon began his main assault on Wellington's army but, after repeated attacks and fierce fighting, failed to overcome the British and was beaten back. The Prussians then attacked from the north-east and the French were routed, losing about half their army and most of their guns. Napoleon reached Paris on 21 June and abdicated on the 22nd. He finally surrendered to the British on 15 July.

After the French defeat, Wellington took a major part in the peace negotiations and was subsequently made commander of the allied occupation army. His command lasted until 15 November 1818, when the armies were evacuated, and he returned to England. The Parliamentary Commissioners had, in 1817, bought for him the estate of Stratfield Saye, in North Hampshire.

The Duke re-entered politics in December 1818, and was made Master-

Silk rosette worn at the Funeral of the Duke of Wellington, 1852

General of the Ordnance, a post which carried Cabinet rank. He was also appointed Lord Lieutenant of Hampshire in December 1820, and Lord High Constable at the Coronation of George IV — an office he later held at the crowning of William IV and Victoria. In September 1822, he took Lord Londonderry's place at the Congress of Verona, where he stood for non-intervention in the affairs of Spain, but failed to persuade his allies.

After a brief mission to Russia in 1826, he was appointed Commander-in-Chief in January 1827, at the same time retaining his Cabinet position; both of which he resigned, however, on 12 April after a dispute with Canning. He was reappointed on 22 August by Lord Goderich, after Canning's death. On 9 January 1828, Wellington became Prime Minister, although he had no desire for the post, and resigned command of the army.

His period of office was a stormy one, and is perhaps best remembered for the difficult but successful passage of the Catholic Emancipation Bill. The Government fell in November 1830. During the Grey administration which followed, the Duke opposed the Reform Bill and became very unpopular with large sections of the public. The windows of Apsley House were broken by a mob on 27 April 1831, and again later on. These occurrences caused him to fit iron shutters to the windows of Apsley House, which remained there until his death. But this unpopularity did not last for long. A happier occasion was his election to the Chancellorship of Oxford University in 1834.

In November 1834 William IV dismissed Melbourne (who had taken Grey's place) and in the Peel administration which followed the Duke served as Foreign Secretary. After four months the Government fell and

Peel and the Duke were again in opposition.

When Peel returned to power in 1841 the Duke (whose health had been failing since 1837) was given a seat in the Cabinet, but without office. On 15 August 1844, he was again appointed Commander-in-Chief, a post he continued to hold after the Peel Government fell in June 1846.

From that time he ceased to take a prominent part in public life, although he once again came into national prominence when he organized the military defence of London against the threat of Chartist riots in April 1848. But he took an informed and active interest in foreign and domestic affairs and he is particularly remembered as an admired, admiring, and almost daily visitor to the Great Exhibition of 1851, where he was once nearly mobbed by an enthusiastic crowd.

On 14 September 1852 he died peacefully at Walmer Castle, Kent, his official residence as Lord Warden of the Cinque Ports. His body lay in state there until 10 November, when it was brought to London. It again lay in state for five days in Chelsea Hospital, where 200,000 people paid homage to the great Duke. The funeral was one of the great spectacles of the century, with over a million and a half people lining the route from the Horse Guards to St Paul's Cathedral, where he was buried on 18 November.

Titles, Offices and Appointments of the Duke

Obelisk with Wellington's orders and titles from the centrepiece of the Prussian Service, Berlin porcelain, about 1819

Ensign, *7 March 1787*

Lieutenant, *25 December 1787*

Captain, *30 June 1791*

Major, *30 April 1793*

Lieut.-Colonel, *30 September 1793*

Colonel, *3 May 1796*

Major-General, *29 April 1802*

Knight Companion of the Bath, *1 September 1804*

Colonel of the 33rd Regiment of Foot (later the Duke of Wellington's Regiment), *30 January 1806 (to December 1812)*

Irish Secretary, *3 April 1807 (resigned April 1809)*

Privy Councillor, *8 April 1807*

Lieutenant-General, *25 April 1808*

Marshal-General of the Portuguese Army, *6 July 1809*

Baron Douro of Wellesley and Viscount Wellington of Talavera, *26 August 1809*

Member of the Regency in Portugal, *August 1810*

General, *31 July 1811*

Conde de Vimieiro and Knight Grand Cross of the Tower and Sword (Portugal), *26 October 1811*

A grandee of Spain, with the title of Duque de Ciudad Rodrigo, *February 1812*

Earl of Wellington, *18 February 1812*

Order of the Golden Fleece (Spain), *1 August 1812*

Generalissimo of the Spanish Armies, *August 1812*

Marquess of Wellington, *18 August 1812*

Marquez de Torres Vedras (Portugal), *August 1812*

Duque da Victoria (Portugal), *18 December 1812*

Colonel of the Royal Regiment of Horse Guards, *1 January 1813 (to 1827)*

Knight of the Garter, *4 March 1813*

Field Marshal, *21 June 1813*

Marquess Douro and Duke of Wellington, *3 May 1814*

Ambassador to the Court of France, *5 July 1814 (to November)*

Prince of Waterloo (Netherlands), *18 July 1815*

Commander-in-Chief of the Allied Armies of Occupation in France, *22 October 1815*

Field Marshal in the Austrian, Russian and Prussian Armies, *October 1818*

Master-General of the Ordnance, *26 December 1818*

Governor of Plymouth, *9 December 1819*

Colonel-in-Chief of the Rifle Brigade, *19 February 1820*

Lord High Constable (at the Coronations of George IV, William IV and Victoria), *1821, 1831, 1838*

Constable of the Tower of London, *29 December 1826*

Colonel of the Grenadier Guards, *22 January 1827*

Commander-in-Chief, *22 January 1827*

Prime Minister, *15 February 1828 (resigned October 1830)*

Lord Warden of the Cinque Ports, *20 January 1829*

Chancellor of the University of Oxford, *30 January 1834*

Secretary of State for Foreign Affairs, *December 1834 (resigned April 1835)*

Master of Trinity House, *22 May 1837*

Ranger of Hyde Park and St James's Park, *31 August 1850*

Miscellany

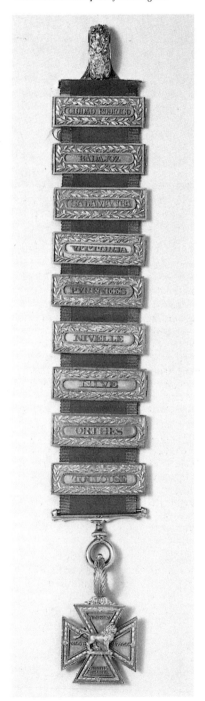

Peninsular Cross, about 1814, the only example with nine clasps, inscribed 'General the Marquis of Wellington'

There is a pillar near Wellington in Somerset, an obelisk in Phoenix Park, Dublin, and a monument by Marochetti outside the gates of Stratfield Saye House. Of the many busts the most interesting are perhaps that by Guillaume (Willem) Geefs (1805-1883) in the village church of Waterloo, that by Nollekens at Apsley House, which the Duke's wife and elder son thought the best likeness, and the one in the guardroom of Windsor Castle, over which hangs a French banner, replaced annually by the Dukes of Wellington on Waterloo Day (18 June) as a condition of the tenure of the estates voted to the Duke by Parliament. Among the many subject paintings in which the Duke figures are the Meeting of *Wellington and Blücher* by T.J. Barker, the wall-painting of the same subject by David Maclise in the Houses of Parliament and Robert Thorburn's large miniature showing the Duke in the library at Stratfield Saye with his grandchildren.

The Duke's funeral on 18 November 1852 was perhaps the most elaborate funeral ever held in this country. It was decided to mount the coffin on an elborate *Triumphal Car*, which was designed and built in some three weeks. It was designed by the Government School of Design (now the Royal College of Art) under the supervision of Henry Cole and Richard Redgrave and was made of the metal of guns captured at Waterloo. It was constructed by eight firms and the great embroidered pall was worked by women students of the School of Design. The six-wheeled car was 20 feet long and 17 feet high (so that, with the added height of coffin and bier, it could just clear Temple Bar) and bore a large Wellington coat of arms on the front and elaborate trophies of actual weapons on the front and sides.

Stretched above the coffin and removable bier was a canopy. The car,

now at Stratfield Saye House, was drawn by twelve black horses along the route from the Horse Guards — whence the body had been moved from Chelsea Hospital, the scene of the lying-in-state — to St Paul's Cathedral by way of the Mall, Buckingham Palace, Hyde Park Corner, Piccadilly, St James's Palace, Pall Mall, Charing Cross, the Strand and Fleet Street. An enormous crowd lined the route and some 20,000 specially invited people were seated in the Cathedral on temporary stands.

The Cathedral was blacked out and the four-hour service took place by the light of gas jets. The coffin and wheeled bier were let down into the crypt exactly under the centre of the dome and placed on top of Nelson's tomb, from which the upper part had been removed. It remained there for a year (until 22 November 1853) by which time the Wellington tomb was ready to receive it. This was placed in the crypt, to the east of Nelson's tomb. The *Tomb* is a simple and massive structure of Cornish porphyry resting on a base of Peterhead granite. It was designed by F. C. Penrose, and finally completed in August 1858.

In 1857 a competition was held for a large *Monument to the Duke* to be placed in the Cathedral proper. The winner was Alfred Stevens, who designed an impressive monument to include both a recumbent effigy and an equestrian figure. The original model is in the Victoria and Albert Museum. But owing to interminable delays and acrimonious controversies the tomb was not finished until 1878; even then it was placed in the south-west Chapel (the present Chapel of St Michael and St George) although designed for the north aisle. It was transferred to its proper position in 1892. Even then it was incomplete, as another — and absurd — controversy had led to the omission of the crowning equestrian figure on the grounds of the unsuitability of allowing a horse in the Cathedral. However, the bronze figure was ultimately completed by John Tweed from the model left by Stevens (who had died in 1875), and was placed in position in 1912. It is the largest monument in St Paul's Cathedral, and the bronze recumbent effigy is particularly fine.

The *Wellington Arms* (see p. 5): quarterly: 1st and 4th gules, a cross argent, between five plates, in saltire, in each quarter, for Wellesley; 2nd and 3rd, or, a lion rampant, gules, for Colley; and as an honourable augmentation, in chief an escutcheon, charged with the crosses of St George, St Andrew, and St Patrick, conjoined, being the union badge of the United Kingdom of Great Britain and Ireland. The *Crest:* out of a ducal coronet, or, a demi-lion rampant gules, holding a forked pennon of the last, flowing to the sinister, one-third per pale from the staff, argent, charged with the cross of St George. The *Supporters:* two lions gules, each gorged with an eastern crown, and chained or. The *Motto* is: *Virtutis Fortuna Comes* (Fortune the Companion of Valour).

The title *"Wellington"* is taken from the manor of Wellington in Somerset which was given to the Duke by the Nation in 1812. The name has been given to countless buildings, streets, squares and open spaces throughout the country — there being twenty-six streets, etc., in the London area alone. The two most famous buildings bearing the Duke's name are Wellington Barracks, London, and Wellington College, Berkshire. *Wellington Barracks,* in Birdcage Walk, was built in 1834 and is the headquarters of the Brigade of Guards. *Wellington College,* which is near Sandhurst, was built by public subscription as a national memorial to the Duke, to form a public school for the sons of officers. The sum of £100,000 was raised, and the first stone

was laid on 2 June 1856 by Queen Victoria, who opened the College on 29 January 1859. The Capital City of New Zealand — Wellington — was named after the Duke on 28 November 1840 by Edward Gibbon Wakefield, the founder of the colony. Also called Wellington are a mountain in Tasmania; three towns and a lake in Australia; a town in Canada; a town in South Africa; a channel in the Arctic regions of Canada; an island off Chile; etc. There have been a number of warships of the Royal Navy named *Duke of Wellington, Wellington,* and *Wellesley;* as well as various merchant ships. The Royal Air Force has had two famous bombers named, respectively, *Wellesley* and *Wellington.*

Wellington Boots were of two kinds — the high boots covering the knees in front and cut away behind, and a shorter kind worn under the trousers. More lately the title has been applied to the familiar high rubber boots. Keats wrote in 1821: "Miss's comb is made a pearl tiara, and common Wellingtons turn Romeo boots." The first printed reference to Wellington boots was by Moncrieff in 1817. The *Wellington Coat* was "a kind of half-and-half great coat and under-coat . . . meeting close and square below the knees" (Creevey, 1828). *Wellington Trousers* were referred to by Sir Walter Scott (1818): "the equally fashionable latitude and longitude of the Wellington trousers." The *Wellington Apple,* a cooking apple, was named by Richard Williams in 1821: "a very handsome and long keeping variety" as the Transactions of the Horticultural Society said in 1822. Perhaps the most distinguished use of the name is the *Wellingtonia,* the popular name in England for the giant Californian sequoia tree, the *sequoia gigantea,* given it by the English botanist John Lindley. The *Gardener's Chronicle* (1853) says: "Wellington stands as high above his contemporaries as the Californian tree above all

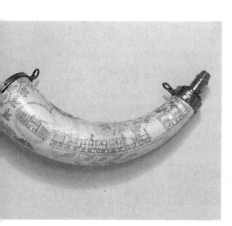

Powder-horn. Lent by the Duke of Wellington

surrounding foresters. Let it then bear henceforward the name of *Wellingtonia gigantea.*"

The name *"Waterloo"* is also popular as a name for streets of which the best known is Waterloo Place — where the Duke had stones erected to assist the clubmen to mount their horses — and there are, of course, Waterloo Station and Waterloo Bridge (the original bridge was opened in 1817); and another Waterloo Bridge across the River Conway in Gwynedd, opened in 1815. There is also the Waterloo Tower, built to commemorate the battle, by Sir Watkin Wynn in Wynnstay Park, Clwyd. In the Cemetery of Brussels, a Waterloo monument was erected, at the wish of Queen Victoria, over the graves of the officers and men who fell in the campaign of 1815. It was unveiled by the Duke of Cambridge, 26 August 1890. It was suggested, and rejected that four London churches projected before 1815 and finished afterwards should be called the 'Waterloo Churches'. The name has stuck although the then Chancellor of the Exchequer stated that "the idea of appropriating churches to commemorate our triumphs did not appear to him to be one that could be entertained". The four churches are: St Matthew's, Brixton; St Mark's, Kennington; St Luke's, Norwood; and St John's, Waterloo Road (damaged by a bomb and rebuilt in 1950 to be the 1951 "Festival Church").

The Waterloo Chamber in Windsor Castle was built in 1830 by George IV to display portraits, mostly by Sir Thomas Lawrence, of those men chiefly responsible for the overthrow of Napoleon, and includes one of the Duke bearing the Sword of State.

The Duke of Wellington never met Napoleon; and met Nelson only once, and that by chance, in September 1805 at the Colonial Office. Nelson was

killed at the Battle of Trafalgar the month after, on 21 October. Napoleon, after his defeat at Waterloo, abdicated on 22 June 1815, and surrendered to Captain F. L. Maitland on 15 July on board H.M.S. *Bellerophon* at Rochefort (France). He was taken in this ship to Plymouth. On 7 August he sailed in H.M.S. *Northumberland* for the island of St Helena where he died on 5 May 1821, at the age of fifty-one.

At the suggestion of the Duke, the *Silver Waterloo Medal* was given "not only to the higher officers, but to all ranks alike, a thing unprecedented".

There is no authority for believing the Duke ever made the oft-quoted exhortation at the Battle of Waterloo, "Up Guards and at them!"; or for his alleged remark that the Battle of Waterloo was won on the playing fields of Eton.

The origin of the words, 'Iron Duke', is uncertain, but the Duke was certainly called this during his lifetime. The earliest known use in print is in *The Mechanics Magazine* in 1845, although *Punch* referred to him in 1842 as "the Wrought-iron Duke". It was long ago suggested that this sobriquet derived from his installation of iron shutters on Apsley House; or, alternatively, that it referred to his face and bearing. Most evidence points to the former origin. Tennyson, in his "Ode" on the Duke's funeral (1852), referred to "their ever-loyal iron leader's fame"; and thereafter the Duke was constantly called the Iron Duke, even in serious works. An earlier reference is another possibility. In 1822 the Duke became deaf in the left ear as a result of an incompetent doctor's attention. He complained saying, "Even the strength of my iron constitution tells now against me." A number of merchant ships have been called *Iron Duke*, although at first the name appears to have been a kind of nickname when iron ships were superseding wood vessels. But two battleships of the Royal Navy have borne the name; the first launched in 1870, the second Admiral Jellicoe's flagship at the Battle of Jutland in 1916, launched in 1912.

The Duke fought one duel, on 21 March 1829, when he was Prime Minister. The Earl of Winchilsea had publicly accused him of dishonesty over the Catholic Emancipation Bill, and was challenged by the Duke. The duel took place at 8 a.m. in Battersea Fields (now Battersea Park). The Duke apparently intended to aim for his opponent's legs but missed: whereupon Lord Winchilsea fired into the air. After which he apologized to the Duke. "I was amazed yesterday morning", wrote Mrs Arbuthnot, "by the Duke walking in while I was at breakfast and telling me he had been fighting Lord Winchilsea . . . The Duke went afterwards to Windsor and saw the King, who thought he was quite right."

Sir Thomas Lawrence (1769-1830), Painting, 1814, Windsor Castle, Waterloo Chamber.

Baron Marochetti (1805-1867), Bronze equestrian statue, 1844, Glasgow.

Count Alfred d'Orsay, Painting, 1845, National Portrait Gallery.

Sir John Steell (1804-1891), bronze equestrian statue, 1852, Edinburgh.

Alfred Stevens (1817-1875), Bronze recumbent effigy and bronze equestrian statue, 1857 (completed by John Tweed (1869-1933)), Wellington Monument, St Paul's Cathedral.

Sir David Wilkie (1785-1841), Painting, 1834, Merchant Taylors' Hall.

Franz Winterhalter (1806-1873), The First of May, 1851, a painting showing the Duke with Queen Victoria, the Prince Consort and the Duke's godson, Prince Arthur, Windsor Castle.

Portraits: a selection of the more important, excluding those at Apsley House:

Sir Joseph Boehm (1834-1890), Bronze equestrian statue, 1846, opposite Apsley House.

Sir Francis Chantrey (1781-1841), Bronze equestrian statue, erected 1844, opposite the Royal Exchange.

Francesco Goya (1746-1828), Painting, 1814, National Gallery.

Benjamin Robert Haydon (1786-1846), Painting, 1839, Stratfield Saye House.

Thomas Heaphy (1775-1835), Drawing, 1813, National Portrait Gallery.

Robert Home (1752-1835), Painting, 1804, National Portrait Gallery.

John Hoppner (1758-1810), Painting, about 1795, Strafield Saye House.

Linked with Apsley House are four familiar monuments.

The *Constitution Hill Arch* was designed by Decimus Burton and erected in 1828 in front of the present entrance to Hyde Park. In 1846 there was placed on it a huge equestrian statue of the Duke of Wellington by M. C. Wyatt. In 1883 the arch was moved to its present position at the top of Constitution Hill, and the statue sent to Aldershot, where it still stands on a knoll near Wellington Avenue. It was not until 1912 that the present group of Peace in a Quadriga (four-horse chariot) by Adrian Jones was placed on it. To replace the Wyatt statue, the present *Equestrian Statue in Bronze*, on a granite base, was placed directly opposite Apsley House in December 1888. The group is the work of Sir J. E. Boehm, R.A. At each corner of the

pedestal stands the figure of a soldier —
a Grenadier, 42nd Royal Highlander,
23rd Royal Welch Fusilier, and 6th
Inniskilling Dragoon. The Duke is
shown on his horse Copenhagen. This
chestnut charger, ridden by the Duke at
Waterloo, was born in 1808. He died 12
February 1836 at Stratfield Saye, and
was buried with military honours. A
headstone marks the grave, inscribed:

*God's humble instrument, though
   meaner clay,
Should share the glory of that
   glorious day.*

The *Achilles* statue, which stands inside
Hyde Park and just to the north-west of
Apsley House, was erected in June
1822. The pedestal bears the
inscription: "To Arthur, Duke of
Wellington, and his brave companions
in arms this statue of Achilles cast from
cannon taken in the victories of
Salamanca, Vitoria, Toulouse and
Waterloo is inscribed by their country-
women." The eighteen-foot statue of
Achilles, by Sir Richard Westmacott, is
a bronze adaptation of one of the
antique Horse-tamer figures on the
Quirinal Hill, Rome. It cost £10,000.

Marble Arch (at the north-east corner of
Hyde Park) was designed by John
Nash, to the order of George IV, both
as a memorial to the victories of
Trafalgar and Waterloo, and as a Royal
entrance to Buckingham Palace. But
the sculptural decorations were not
included when the arch was erected in
front of the Palace in 1833; they were
incorporated instead in the exterior of
the Palace itself, and the arch was no
longer regarded as a victory memorial.
It was transferred to its present position
in 1851. The original model, with
scenes not only of Waterloo but of the
Duke receiving the Order of the Garter
(the latter sculpture never being carried
out), is in the Victoria and Albert
Museum.

The Paintings

In 1812 the Intendant of Segovia, in recognition of Wellington's liberation of Spain from the French, gave him twelve paintings from the Palace of Ildefonso. The final expulsion of the French from Spain followed Wellington's victory at the battle of Vitoria on 21 June 1813. After that battle Joseph Bonaparte, who had been made King of Spain in 1808, fled. His coach was captured and proved to contain over 200 paintings appropriated from the Spanish Royal Collections. They had been detached from their stretchers and rolled up. Wellington sent them to London to the custody of his brother, Lord Maryborough. In 1814, when they had been catalogued and their importance and royal provenance discovered, Wellington not only had them restored but also offered to return them to the King of Spain. A further offer in 1816 produced the response from Count Fernan Nunez, Spanish Minister in England that: "His Majesty, touched by your delicacy, does not wish to deprive you of that which has come into your possession by means as just as they are honourable".

Eighty-three of these paintings are now at Apsley House. They range in date from the Juan de Flandes Last Supper, which was painted for Queen Isabella of Castille before her death in 1504, to the Mengs Holy Family dated 1765, and include works by such masters as Correggio, Elsheimer, Rubens, Velazquez, and Van Dyck.

After the end of the war the Duke bought some important old master paintings, mainly Dutch, in Paris at the La Peyrière sale (April 1817) and the Le Rouge sale (April 1818) and from the dealer, painter and restorer, Féréol Bonnemaison (1818). From the same period onwards he also collected modern portraits of his comrades-in-arms by Lawrence, and others, and portraits of Napoleon and his family

mainly by Lefèvre. Portraits of the allied sovereigns came as gifts. Wellington's most important modern purchase was Wilkie's Chelsea Pensioners, commissioned in 1816. The second Duke of Wellington also collected; seven of the two hundred pictures at Apsley House were acquired by him.

In recent years a programme has been underway to rehang the paintings following, insofar as possible, their arrangement under the first Duke, as recorded in descriptions and watercolours. As a result many of the paintings have been restored to the rooms where they were hung by the first Duke and several are close to their original positions. The first Duke probably had about ninety more paintings than are now in the rooms on view at Apsley House; their arrangement was therefore even richer and denser. The frames are all as supplied to the first Duke: his principal framemaker was Thomas Temple after whose bankruptcy in 1839 Robert Thick was employed.

The Last Supper, with the institution of the Eucharist and Christ washing the Disciples' feet, by Juan de Flandes. One of a series of 47 panels which belonged to Queen Isabella of Spain (died 1504).

† This symbol is used to indicate a painting captured at the Battle of Vitoria, 1813.
* This symbol is used to indicate that the painting is known to have hung in the same room under the 1st Duke of Wellington.